FUNCTIONAL PROGRAM
TESTING AND ANALYSIS

FUNCTIONAL PROGRAM TESTING AND ANALYSIS

William E. Howden
University of California at San Diego

McGraw-Hill Book Company

New York   St. Louis   San Francisco   Auckland   Bogotá   Hamburg
London   Madrid   Mexico   Milan   Montreal   New Delhi
Panama   Paris   São Paulo   Singapore   Sydney   Tokyo   Toronto

This book was set in Times Roman by Publication Services.
The editors were Karen M. Jackson and Joseph F. Murphy;
the designer was Joan E. O'Connor;
the production supervisor was Denise L. Puryear.
Project supervision was done by Publication Services.
R.R. Donnelley & Sons Company was printer and binder.

FUNCTIONAL PROGRAM TESTING AND ANALYSIS

1234567890 DOCDOC 89210987

ISBN 0-07-030550-1

Library of Congress Cataloging-in-Publication Data
Howden, William E.
    Functional program testing and analysis.

    (Software engineering series)
    1. Computer programs—Testing.   I. Title.
II. Series: Software engineering series (New York, N.Y.)
QA76.6.H7   1987   005.3'028'7   86-28220
ISBN 0-07-030550-1

For Becky, Amos and Cricket

For Becky, Amos and Cricket

CONTENTS

PREFACE

Testing is an unavoidable part of any responsible effort to develop a software system. Over the past 15 years more and more attention has been given to this topic, but it is still a relatively new one and has consisted primarily of an unintegrated collection of methods whose justification is intuitive rather than scientific or mathematical.

This book presents an integrated approach to program testing and analysis which has a sound mathematical basis. It describes both previous techniques, and how they fit together, as well as new methods. It provides a general approach to testing and validation that incorporates all important software life cycle products, including requirements and general and detailed designs. The theory part of the book contains mathematical results that can be used to characterize the effectiveness of different functional testing and analysis methods. The results can be used to prove that well-defined classes of faults and failures will be discovered by specific techniques. Functional testing and analysis is a general approach to verification and validation and not only integrates current techniques, but indicates fruitful directions for continued research and development.

This book is written for the practicing software engineer and for the advanced undergraduate or graduate student. Although some familiarity with basic software engineering concepts would be useful, all of the related ideas are explained. This includes material on requirements and on general and detailed design. The theoretical foundations part of the book relies on several branches of mathematics, and all of this material is also fully explained.

If used as a text, the book is suitable for courses in software engineering or in testing and validation. For a general course on software engineering it is recommended that it be used along with a good book on design or a general software engineering text that covers design methodology in depth.

The book has three major sections. The first section consists of the first three chapters. It contains a discussion of functions, states, and types in programs and illustrates their central role in requirements, design, and coding with two detailed examples. The second section contains the fourth chapter and includes the theoretical foundations which are used to put functional testing and analysis on a sound mathematical basis. This section outlines a theory of testing based on fault and failure analysis, and contains results in statistics, algebra, and graph theory. The basic concepts of the first and second sections are combined to produce the systematic approach to testing and analysis described in the third section, consisting of Chapters 5, 6, and 7.

It is not necessary for the reader to learn all of the mathematical results in the fourth chapter in order to apply functional testing and analysis. It is possible to skip most of this chapter and then only to look back at selected material referenced in Chapters 5 and 6. The exception is Sections 4.1 and 4.2, which should be read after Chapters 1, 2, and 3, and before going on to Chapters 5 through 7. Section 4.2 describes the basic integrating concepts used to build the systematic testing methodology that is detailed in the remaining chapters of the book.

Many of the methods described in the book depend on the use of software tools for support. A complete collection of functional testing and analysis tools is under construction and additional information about them is available from *Critical Software Systems*, P.O. Box 1241, Solana Beach, California 92075.

I would like to take this opportunity to thank all of my professional colleagues in software engineering, with whom I have had many insightful conversations. I would like to thank Patrick Dymond, Michael Fredman and Elias Masry at UCSD for discussions on different aspects of the theoretical material. The research upon which this book is based was funded by the Office of Naval Research, and I would like to thank the ONR for their continued support. I would also like to thank Chiquita Payne for her dedication and patience in typing the manuscript and Sue Sullivan who worked on earlier drafts of the material. Finally, I would like to acknowledge my dependence on that source of all creativity and knowledge from whom I have derived what modest inspiration guided the writing of this book.

William E. Howden
Solana Beach, California

FUNCTIONAL PROGRAM
TESTING AND ANALYSIS

FUNCTIONAL PROGRAM
TESTING AND ANALYSIS

CHAPTER

1

INTRODUCTION

1.1 TESTING

Testing is a fundamental part of all branches of engineering, and it is an essential part of software development. In manufacturing processes that involve physical products, testing is carried out to detect materials defects. In software development all errors are human errors, and it is tempting to hope that errors can be eliminated with better development methods, better trained programmers, or some kind of programming language or environment that proves to be a universal panacea for human fallibility. However, there is no reason to believe that this will ever be the case, except in special circumstances, and testing will continue to play a major role in software engineering.

1.2 TESTING AND THE SOFTWARE LIFE CYCLE

In the modern life-cycle approach to software development, a variety of documents are produced before and during software development which make the process less error-prone and more systematic. Life-cycle software development may include requirements analysis methods such as data-flow analysis,[1] specification systems such as Problem Statement Language/Problem Statement Analysis (PSL/PSA),[2] general design methods such as Structured Design[3] and Structural Analysis and Design Technique (SADT)[4] and detailed design techniques such as Program Design Languages[5] and Nassi-Schneiderman diagrams.[6]

1

The advantage of systematic life-cycle development is that it reduces complexity by separating the description of different aspects of a software system into parts. This simplifies the description and makes software development easier and more systematic. It enables the detection of basic errors earlier in the development process and decreases the cost of their elimination.

The approach to testing outlined in this book uses the information about a system which is contained in a typical set of life-cycle documents. The approach can also be applied, but less easily, to a system which consists only of programs and no other documents.

1.3 TESTING, HIGH-LEVEL LANGUAGES, AND SPECIFICATIONS

One way to reduce errors in programs is to use high-level languages, or languages which are specialized for particular areas of application. This reduces errors by reducing the logical complexity of the object that must be created by a programmer. The use of very high-level languages is feasible in applications areas where large numbers of very similar programs are required, and new programs can be constructed by providing the system specification in some tabular format. There are a variety of commercial data processing program construction systems like this, in which all the user has to do is specify file or data-base formats. This is the only place in which testing can, foreseeably, become unnecessary, but it is because there is no programming being done.

Ideally, it may appear that a general purpose formal specifications language could be developed which would allow the specification of any program, and that testing would become unnecessary because the program would be generated mechanically from the specification and hence be correct. This is an unlikely possibility. If the specifications language were general purpose, then the programmer would have to specify as much logical information in the specification as he previously had to in a program, and the net result would be that the errors would be in the specification now instead of the program. In principle, such a specifications language would be a kind of programming language, possibly a worse one than a conventional language, and no real problem would be solved by its use. The success with high-level specifications languages for data processing systems is the result of specialization rather than specification.

If a family of specialized specification systems could be developed that would have the advantages of the data processing specification systems, then errors and testing would become less important for the applications systems analyst. But this would be because he would no longer really be a programmer. The programming would be in the construction of the translator which transformed the specifications into programs, and testing would play its traditional, necessary role here.

1.4 TESTING AND PROOFS OF CORRECTNESS

It has often been quoted that "testing can only be used to detect the presence of bugs, not to prove their absence." The implication is that testing should be abandoned and some form of proof method adopted. Before going into the limitations of proofs it should be pointed out that testing has some very important advantages over proof methods.

There is no such thing as an absolute proof of correctness; there are only proofs of equivalency. Program proofs of correctness are proofs that one description of a function is equivalent to another. Usually, one is a state description in a formal logical language and the other is an algorithm description in a programming language. It often happens during software development that it is necessary to invent some expression or function to carry out a computation whose full specification is not yet available. A few selected cases may be known, and a computational procedure constructed that is characterized by those cases. After the experimental period, based on testing, it will be possible to construct a more complete specification.

The dependency of proofs on formal specifications is a pervasive difficulty in the attempt to use proofs of correctness. Formal specifications for combinatorial or mathematical programs may be concise and may clearly describe the intended computational effect of a program, but for other programs this is often not the case. There are many programs for which formal specifications are artificial and obscure, and much more difficult to construct, read, and understand than the specified program. Formal specifications describe initial and final states of a system in terms of relationships between variables. Programs are transformers which change initial states to final states. For many programs there is no reasonable way to express relationships between initial and final states except in the form of the program which establishes the relationship.

Another factor that inhibits the use of proofs of correctness is the difficulty of constructing a program proof. It is a tedious, error-prone task, consisting of many cases and inductions. Techniques have been developed to simplify the proof process, but proofs may be longer and more difficult to understand than the proved programs. In addition, proofs of correctness are usually proofs of the correctness of the logic of an algorithm and not of programs. The peculiarities of fixed length word sizes, floating point numbers, and other computer dependent properties are ignored. If they were not, the proofs would become even more detailed and difficult to understand.

Although, in principle, it may be possible to prove the correctness of a program, it may simply not be cost efficient. There is often a sense of urgency in software development. A usable product must be completed within a time frame that will not allow formal specification and proof. No added value would be introduced into the system or program by formal specifications and proofs, even if this were to increase its relative mean time between failure from 75 to 100 percent.

Continuing research in program proving will expand the scope of applicability of and ease of use of proofs. For a variety of reasons, however, it is unlikely that proofs will replace testing. Perhaps the most fruitful area of application for proofs of correctness is in the design stage, where they can be used to prove that certain general algorithmic concepts have some desired property. Such proofs may be independent of the eventual structure of a program and use traditional mathematical techniques, such as proof by contradiction, that are difficult to use when proofs are tied to program structure. Once the basic design ideas are proved, then testing and analysis can be used to confirm that a designed and implemented program conforms to those ideas. Both proving and testing are considered to have their place, and their cooperative use should continue to increase.

1.5   FUNCTIONAL TESTING AND ANALYSIS

Current Institute of Electrical and Electronics Engineers (IEEE) standards define a bug in a program as a *fault* and the incorrect behavior of the program induced by the fault as a *failure*. This terminology will be used throughout the book.

Testing has traditionally been unsystematic and unreliable because there was no unifying approach to combining different testing methods and no theory to characterize the classes of faults and failures that could be found by different methods. This book describes such an approach. The basic idea is that programs can be viewed as collections of functions which are synthesized from other functions, and that program faults correspond to faults in synthesis. There are two very general ways of joining functions together—functional synthesis and structural synthesis.

In *functional synthesis*, expressions and other simple programming constructs are used to construct an input-output function. The programmer may not know the specification of the new function but is expected to know what the correct output would be for selected input. General classes of functional synthesis faults are defined, along with the kinds of tests needed to reveal those faults. *Functional testing* involves the testing of functions formed by functional synthesis over fault revealing test data. It is called functional testing since the emphasis is on execution of functions and examination of their input and output data.

In *structural synthesis*, functions are joined together into graph-like structures which describe the sequences in which they should be executed. Failures correspond to wrong sequences of function invocation or to wrong transmission of data between one function and another. *Functional analysis* involves the analysis of programs for structural synthesis failures. In some cases failures can be detected by the presence of inconsistent data interfaces, and in others the programmer is expected to have a description of correct function usage sequences.

Functional testing is a fault analysis method since it depends on the definition and detection of specified classes of faults. In functional testing the programmer exhaustively tests for classes of faults. Exhaustive testing for all possible failures is not possible since the number of different possible input-output pairs that would have to be examined is prohibitively large. Exhaustive testing for classes of faults is feasible since the number of different possible commonly occurring classes of functional synthesis faults is relatively small. Functional analysis is a failure analysis rather than a fault analysis method since it involves looking for all possible structural synthesis failures, that is, failures in function sequencing. This is feasible since it is possible to prove that if there are any such failures, they will occur in a small finite set of sequences which can be exhaustively examined. Functional analysis is more powerful in this sense, since it can detect the presence of any fault which results in a function sequence failure. Functional testing can detect only failure-causing faults for which it has been possible to construct fault-testing rules. This may leave kinds of failures not caused by those classes of faults undetected.

1.6 VERIFICATION AND VALIDATION

The words verification and validation are often used in discussing testing and analysis, although they are used in a variety of contradictory and confusing ways. The entire process of examining a software product to confirm that it operates as intended is often referred to as "V and V" without any attempt to explain what the differences between the two words are or why two words are even necessary. The word verification is sometimes associated uniquely with proofs of correctness.

The following definitions are consistent with the original way in which these two words were used. *Verification* refers to the activity of comparing a software development product with some description of that product that occurred earlier in the development process. General designs may be verified with respect to requirements analysis documents, detailed designs with respect to general designs, and programs with respect to detailed designs. When the only development products are specifications and programs, then programs are verified by comparing them with their specifications. This is consistent with the use of the word verification to refer to proofs of correctness, in which programs are proved equivalent to formal specifications.

Validation means to compare a software development product with the user's perceived requirements for that product. The term is sometimes used to refer to customer acceptance testing when the final software system is tested in the environment for which it was intended. Other products besides code can be validated. Requirements and design products may be compared directly with user expectations through the use of prototypes or simulation.

Functional testing and analysis methods can be used for both verification and validation and in this book are not organized into separate sections based on this classification. They can be used with different life-cycle products, involving information from requirements, general design, detailed design, and coding.

1.7 TOOLS

Many of the testing and analysis methods which will be discussed depend on the availability of tools. The basic features of such tools are described and some of the currently available tools are referenced.

1.8 ORGANIZATION OF THE BOOK

The remaining part of the book begins with a discussion of functions, states, and types. Functions and states are considered to be the basic concepts in a system, and their occurrence in requirements, general and detailed designs, and code is discussed. This is followed by a chapter on the theoretical foundations of functional testing and analysis. The basic ideas of testing and analysis are discussed along with the fundamental mathematical results upon which the method is based.

The first part of the theoretical foundations chapter contains a discussion of the impossibility of proving correctness by testing. This is followed by a discussion of what can be proved. Sections on statistical testing, algebraic foundations for functional testing, and graph theory foundations for functional analysis are included.

The next two chapters in the book describe functional testing and functional analysis. The application of the basic theoretical results to practical functional testing methods is described in the first of these two chapters. The second describes module and structural interface analysis, the basic techniques of functional analysis.

The final chapter is on the planning and management of software testing. It contains advice on the selection and use of testing and analysis methods. Three software quality assurance packages are suggested, ranging from an inexpensive, manual approach to an expensive, fully automated approach.

REFERENCES

1. T. DeMarco, *Structured Analysis and System Specification*, Yourdon Press, N.Y., 1978.
2. D. Teichroew and E. Hershey, PSL/PSA—Computer aided techniques for structure and

documentation and analysis of information processing systems, *IEEE Transactions on Software Engineering*, SE-6, 1980.

3. E. Yourdon and L. Constantine, *Structured Design*, Prentice-Hall, Englewood Cliffs, N.J., 1979.
4. D. T. Ross, Structured Analysis (SA): A language for communicating ideas, *IEEE Transactions on Software Engineering*, SE-3, January 1977.
5. S. H. Caine and K. E. Gordon, PDL—A tool for software design, *Proceedings National Computer Conference*, vol. 44, 1975.
6. I. Nassi and B. Schneiderman, Flowchart techniques for structured programming, *ACM Sigplan Notices*, 8, 1973.

CHAPTER
2

FUNCTIONS

2.1 FUNCTIONS AND DATA TYPES

Mathematically, all functions are of the form $f: a \rightarrow b$ where f is a function which, for every object of type a, returns an object of type b. In the simplest cases, types are sets of simple objects, such as integers or reals, and in more complex cases they are structured objects having different components.

In defining a function, the data which it operates on and which it produces may be discussed either directly in terms of types or indirectly in terms of properties of variables and data structures used to store data of a specified type. The latter is more common in the more detailed phases of software development, when it becomes necessary to choose variables and data structures.

2.2 SOFTWARE DEVELOPMENT AND FUNCTIONS

Functions and their data are the basic conceptual units that are used to build software. They are used not only in programs but also to construct requirements, and general and detailed designs. They may be both formally and informally defined. The central role of functions in software development is illustrated in the following sections. In the first section, the functions in the informal requirements for a data processing system and the functions in the formal specification for a scientific program are described. This is followed by sections describing the functions in the general and detailed designs for these examples.

It is not necessary for the reader to understand the examples in complete detail. The point is to illustrate how function and data-type definitions arise in and are critical concepts in all phases of software development.

2.3 FUNCTIONS AND REQUIREMENTS

In the first of the following examples, Structured Analysis is used to give an informal set of requirements for a computerized dating system. In the second, mathematical formulae are used to give formal specifications for a scientific program. These two examples are representative of the variety of methods that can be used to provide preliminary descriptions of a proposed program. In general, requirements will be informal for systems and programs that are new and are not translations of previously constructed programs, or for translations from a formal noncomputational logical language, such as mathematics, to a computational one.

The purpose of the examples is to illustrate the central role of functions in requirements and to show how their presence can be easily identified in Structured Analysis documents.

2.3.1 Dating System Example

In Structured Analysis[1] the requirements for a system are described using data-flow diagrams and data dictionaries. The method is commonly used to describe the requirements for data processing systems. Data-flow diagrams consist of arcs, which represent data flow, and nodes, which represent data transformations. Figure 2.1 contains the data-flow diagram for a computerized dating system. The system is expected to find the best date in its database for individual clients. Clients and dates are part of the same population and each client's dating information is expected to be in the *datefile* database. The information stored for each date consists of the personal and physical characteristics of the date as well as the personal and physical

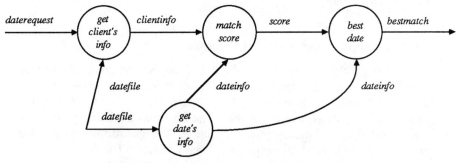

FIGURE 2.1.   Data-flow diagram for dating system.

characteristics which the date likes. These form the *dater* and *datee* information for each potential client or dater. The best match is computed by finding, for a client, the date for which the client and the date best satisfy each other's likes. The system also contains a deletion process for removing dates from the system and an insertion process for adding dates, but this will be excluded from the discussion.

Four major functions can be recognized in the data-flow diagram for the dating system example: *getclientsinfo, matchscore, getdatesinfo,* and *bestdate*. In addition, there is an implicit database access function.

The type of data associated with each function is also described in the data-flow diagram. The *getclientsinfo* function takes a *daterequest* type of data object and *datefile* type data and generates *clientinfo* data. Similarly, the *getdatesinfo* retrieves *dateinfo* data for potential dates from the *datefile* database. The *matchscore* function will take instances of *clientinfo* and *dateinfo* types of data and generate a *score* for a potential date. The *bestdate* function keeps track of the best date so far. It takes *score* and *dateinfo* types of data and eventually generates a *bestmatch* data object.

Different standards can be used for data-flow diagrams. In this book each data-flow diagram node may have one or more input arcs, except for input transformation nodes. If a data transformation node has more than one input arc, the convention is used that there is an implicit "and" of the input data. It transforms the collective "and" of the input into the output data. Data transformation nodes may also have more than one output arc, in which case there is an implicit "or" of the output data types. The data transformation transforms its input data into one of the different possible output types. The exception to this is when there is more than one output arc having the same data name on it. In this case there is conceptually only one arc and one kind of data, which is being sent to different locations.

Data dictionaries can be used to describe relationships between different data flows and the kinds of data they contain. Figure 2.2 contains a dictionary for the *dateinfo* data object. The $\wedge$ symbol means "and" and is used to indicate a compound structure. The $\vee$ symbol means "or" and is used to indicate alternatives.

2.3.2 *covar* Statistics Program Example

In this example the formal specification for a statistical program called *covar* is given. The specified program is capable of processing m sets of observations on n random variables $x(i,j)$, $1 \leq i \leq m$, $1 \leq j \leq n$, to produce the means, cross products, and covariance. The functions computed by the program are defined by mathematical formulae. The specification is divided into three parts: input data, output data, and formulae. The functions computed by the program are explicitly identified in the formulae section of the specifications.

dateinfo → *dater* ∧ *datee*
dater → *id* ∧ *sex* ∧ *religion* ∧ *occupation*
      ∧ *politics* ∧ *daterweight* ∧ *daterheight*
sex → *m* ∨ *f*
religion → *moslem* ∨ *buddhist* ∨ *christian* ∨ *hindu* ∨ *other*
politics → *conservative* ∨ *moderate* ∨ *liberal*
id → *integer*
daterheight → *integer*
daterweight → *integer*
datee → *sex* ∧ *religion* ∧ *occupation*
      ∧ *politics* ∧ *dateeweight* ∧ *dateeheight*
dateeweight → (*integer, integer*)
dateeheight → (*integer, integer*)

FIGURE 2.2. Dating system data dictionary.

A. Input data.
  1. *n*: an integer specifying the number of variables whose observations are being analyzed.
  2. *m*: an integer specifying the number of observations per variable.
  3. *datafile*: the file of observations. In the case of a Fortran program, *datafile* could be the device number for a file. *datafile* contains at least *m* observations on each of *n* variables. Each observation $x(i,j)$, $1 \le i \le m$, $1 \le j \le n$, is a floating-point number. If there are more than *m* observations, only the first *m* are used. If there are less, an error message is generated.
  4. *cvf*: covariance flag. If *cvf* = 0, the covariances of the observations will be calculated. Otherwise the corrected cross products will be calculated.

B. Output data.
  1. *mean(i)*, $1 \le i \le n$: variable means. *mean( )* is used to return the mean value for each observation variable.
  2. *vcv(i,j)*, $1 \le i \le n$, $1 \le j \le n$: corrected cross products and covariances. *vcv( )* contains cross products or covariances, depending on *cvf*.
  3. *err*: error message.

C. Formulae.
  1. Means function. *meanf(datafile)* → *mean*. *mean(j)* is set to the mean of the observations for variable x_j and is computed using the formula:

$$mean(j) = \sum_{i=1}^{m} x(i,j)/m$$

  2. Cross products, covariance function. *crossprf(datafile,cvf,mean)* → *vcv*. If *cvf* ≠ 0, *vcv* will contain the corrected sums of squares and cross products for the data in *datafile*. Otherwise, if *cvf* = 0, *vcv* will contain the covariance matrix. The formulae that are used are:

Cross products:

$$vcv(h,k) = \sum_{i=1}^{m} \sum_{j=1}^{n} (x(i,h) - mean\ (h)) * (x(j,k) - mean(k))$$

Covariance:

$$vcv(h,k) = \sum_{i=1}^{m} \sum_{j=1}^{n} (x(i,h) - mean(h)) * (x(j,k) - mean(k))/(m - 1)$$

2.4   FUNCTIONS AND GENERAL DESIGN

In the design of a program or system new functions are introduced. This can occur because the design is more detailed than the requirements or because, in figuring out how a system will work, the designer needs to add new computational processes. The occurrence of design functions will be illustrated using the Structured Design general design method.

In Structured Design[2] the programmer divides up a system into a collection of interacting modules. The method includes notational conventions for describing modules and their interrelationships, along with rules for evaluating the quality of a design. High-quality designs consist of modules that have a high degree of functional cohesion and a low degree of inter-module data coupling.

The basic notational convention in Structured Design is a top-down, tree-like structure, called a *structure diagram*, in which the nodes correspond to modules and the arcs to relationships between modules. In addition, arcs may have data-flow labels, called *couples*, to show the flow of data between modules.

Although structure diagrams are primarily tools for outlining the broad modular architecture of a system, they can also be used for individual programs. In the following examples, they are used to show structural relationships between the subfunctions that occur as part of the *dater* and *covar* functions in the dating system and *covar* statistics examples. The designs consist of three parts: the data, the functions, and a structure diagram. In both examples the central importance of functions is obvious.

Some of the functions in the examples use or produce more than one kind of data. The notation $a \vee b$ indicates *type a* or *type b* data; $a \wedge b$ indicates *type a* and *type b* data (i.e., a compound data object).

2.4.1   Dating System Example

A. Data.
1. *daterequest*. A client's request for a date.
2. *clientid*. A client's identifier.
3. *clientinfo*. A client's personal data record from the database.
4. *nocl*. A message indicating that a client's data record was not found in the database.

5. *dateinfo*. A date's date record from the database.
6. *eof*. An indicator that when the file is accessed sequentially the end of file has been reached.
7. *bdate*. The best date found so far (i.e., the *dateinfo* of the best date).
8. *bscore*. The highest date score of all the dates examined so far.
9. *score*. The date score for the current date under examination.
10. *better*. An indicator used to determine whether *score* or *bscore* is higher.
11. *bestmatch*. The best date for a client (i.e., the final value of *bdate*).

B. Functions.

1. $dater(daterequest) \rightarrow nocl \lor bestmatch$. The *bestmatch* date finding function.
2. $getrequest \rightarrow daterequest$. Accepts a request for a date from a client.
3. $getdt(clientid) \rightarrow clientinfo \lor nocl$. Retrieves the *clientinfo* record from the database for a client. If there is no record for this client, it returns a *nocl* message.
4. $getnextdt \rightarrow dateinfo \lor eof$. A sequential access function for the database. The first time it is called it initializes and reads from the beginning of the database. Subsequently it returns the next record or an *eof* indicator.
5. $updt(clientinfo,dateinfo,bdate,bscore) \rightarrow bdate \land bscore$. The *updt* function updates the values of bdate and bscore.
6. $blissf(clientinfo,dateinfo) \rightarrow score$. Calculates the match count for two records of dating information.
7. $scrcompare(score,bscore) \rightarrow better$. Indicates whether or not the score just computed for the current date candidate (*score*) is higher than the highest score so far (*bscore*).

C. Structure diagram. The structure diagram for *dater* is contained in Figure 2.3.

In order to simplify the structure diagram the convention has been used that downward data flow is denoted on the left of the structure diagram arcs and upward data flow on the right. The numbers used to indicate data correspond to the numbers in the given listing of the data. The diagram indicates, for example, that the *dater* function sends *clientid*, client identifier data, to the *getdt* function and gets *clientinfo* and *nocl* data in return. In this case either a *clientinfo* or a *nocl* data object is returned, as opposed to both a *clientinfo* and a *nocl* data object, but this is not distinguished in the structure diagram.

2.4.2 *covar* Statistics Program Example

In scientific programs, the design is often based on formulae in which an expression is decomposed or transformed. In the *covar* example, mathematical formulae are used to break the computation into stages. The design decom-

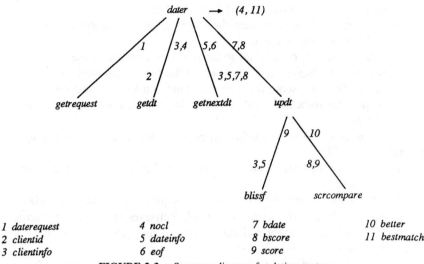

1 *daterequest*   4 *nocl*   7 *bdate*   10 *better*
2 *clientid*   5 *dateinfo*   8 *bscore*   11 *bestmatch*
3 *clientinfo*   6 *eof*   9 *score*

FIGURE 2.3.   Structure diagram for dating system.

position results in the introduction of new functions and data. In each stage of the decomposition, part of the data is processed to generate a partial mean and a partial variance-covariance. In the following formulae, *nmblks* is the number of blocks into which the data is decomposed. The size of block *k*, $1 \leq k \leq nmblks$, is denoted by *szblk(k)*. The notation *x(k,i,j)* is used to indicate observation *(i,j)* in the *k*th block of data.

$$mean(j) = \sum_{i=1}^{m} x(i,j)/m = \sum_{k=1}^{nmblks} \sum_{i=1}^{szblk(k)} x(k,i,j)/m$$

$$vcv(h,j) = (\sum_{i=1}^{m} (x(i,h) - mean(h)) * (x(i,j) - mean(j)))/(m-1)$$

$$= (\sum_{k=1}^{nmblks} \sum_{i=1}^{szblk(k)} (x(k,i,h) - mean(h)) * (x(k,i,j) - mean(j)))/(m-1)$$

In order to prevent multiplication overflow/underflow, the design for *covar* calls for the use of scaling factors. In the following formulae, *sfac(j)*, $1 \leq j \leq n$, denotes the scaling factor for variable *j*. The formulae suggest a more elaborate decomposition of the *covar* computations in which it is possible to first compute the "unadjusted observations cross product" matrix. This is then adjusted for the mean and finally transformed into a variance-covariance. The unadjusted cross products correspond to the first term in the last formula that follows. The unadjusted cross products are adjusted for the mean by subtracting off the second term in the formula. The adjusted cross products are transformed into the variance-covariance by division by the third term, $(m-1)$.

Let $y(k,i,j) = x(k,i,j) - sfac(j)$. Then

$$vcv(h,j) = (\sum_{k=1}^{nmblks} \sum_{i=1}^{szblk(k)} (x(k,i,h) - mean(h)) * (x(k,i,j) - mean(j)))/(m - 1)$$

$$= (\sum_{k=1}^{nmblks} \sum_{i=1}^{szblk(k)} (y(k,i,h) - (mean(h) - sfac(h))) * (y(k,i,j)$$

$$- (mean(j) - sfac(j))))/(m - 1)$$

$$= (\sum_{k=1}^{nmblks} \sum_{i=1}^{szblk(k)} y(k,i,h) * y(k,i,j)$$

$$- \sum_{k=1}^{nmblks} \sum_{i=1}^{szblk(k)} y(k,i,h) * (mean(j) - sfac(j))$$

$$- \sum_{k=1}^{nmblks} \sum_{i=1}^{szblk(k)} y(k,i,j) * (mean(h) - sfac(h))$$

$$+ m * (mean(h) - sfac(h)) * (mean(j) - sfac(j)))/(m - 1)$$

$$= ((\sum_{k=1}^{nmblks} \sum_{i=1}^{szblk(k)} y(k,i,h) * y(k,i,j)) - m * (mean(h) - sfac(h))$$

$$* (mean(j) - sfac(j)))/(m - 1)$$

A. Data.

1. *cvf*. A Boolean variable that indicates whether or not the routine is to return the variance-covariance or the adjusted cross products.
2. *sf*. A Boolean variable that indicates whether the scaling factors are to be found in the first set of observations or are stored in *sfac(i)*, $1 \le i \le n$.
3. *sfac(i)*, $1 \le i \le n$. If *sf* indicates it, *sfac* contains scaling factors to be used in the computations. Otherwise, *sfac* will be computed from the first set of observations.
4. *m*. The maximum number of observations that will be read. If there are more than *m* observations, only the first *m* will be used. If there are less than *m*, an error message *err* will be output and no computed statistics are returned.
5. *err*. An error message indicating inadequate data.
6. *block*. A block of variable observations ($x(k,i,j)$, $1 \le i \le szblk(k)$, $1 \le j \le n$) from *datafile*.
7. *szblk*. The number of observations in the current block of data.
8. *datafile*. The input file of data.
9. *eof*. A Boolean variable indicating that the last *block* in *datafile* has been read.
10. *datum*. A set of variable observations.

11. *eod*. A Boolean variable indicating that m observations have been read from the *datafile*.
12. *psum(i)*, $1 \le i \le n$. A running partial sum for each of the variable observations. In each stage of the computation the observation values in *block* are added to *psum*.
13. *pucp(i,j)*, $1 \le i \le m$, $1 \le j \le n$. A running partial unadjusted cross products matrix.
14. *sum(i)*, $1 \le i \le n$. The total sums of the observations for each variable.
15. *ucp(i,j)*, $1 \le i \le m$, $1 \le j \le n$. The total unadjusted cross products for each pair of variables.
16. *mean(i)*, $1 \le i \le n$. The mean of the observations for each variable.
17. *acp(i,j)*, $1 \le i \le m$, $1 \le j \le n$. The total adjusted cross products for each pair of variables.
18. *vcv(i,j)*, $1 \le i \le m$, $1 \le j \le n$. The variance-covariance matrix for the observed variables.

B. Functions.

1. *covar(cvf,sf,sfac,m,datafile)* $\rightarrow$ *(mean* $\wedge$ *(acp* $\wedge$ *vcv))* $\vee$ *err. covar* uses the input data to compute the *mean* and either the adjusted cross products, *acp*, or the variance-covariance, *vcv*, for the observations in *datafile*. It may also return an error message.
2. *infile(m,datafile)* $\rightarrow$ *(block* $\wedge$ *szblk)* $\vee$ *eod* $\vee$ *eof*. When invoked, *infile* reads a sequence of records from the file one at a time until it has a complete block of records, the end of the file is reached, or m records have been read. It keeps track of how many records it puts in the block and returns this value in *szblk*. In fact, *szblk* is always the same for each block except possibly the last block of records.
3. *indata(m)* $\rightarrow$ *datum* $\vee$ *eod* $\vee$ *eof*. This function reads the next set of observations from the current block. If the block is "used up," it tries to read in another block using *infile*. If *infile* reaches the end of the file before it has read m records, it immediately returns an *eof* to *indata*, which returns it to *covar*, which then terminates with the appropriate error message.
4. *update(datum,psum,pucp,sfac)* $\rightarrow$ *psum* $\wedge$ *pucp*. The *update* function uses *datum* to update the current values of *psum* and *pucp*.
5. *psumf(psum,datum)* $\rightarrow$ *psum*. Updates the partial sum values in *psum* from the data in *datum*.
6. *pucpf(pucp,datum,sfac)* $\rightarrow$ *pucp*. Updates the partial unadjusted cross products in *pucp* using *datum*.
7. *meanvcvf(m,sum,ucp,sfac ,cvf)* $\rightarrow$ *mean* $\wedge$ *(acp* $\vee$ *vcv)*. The mean and either the *acp* or *vcv*, depending on *cvf*, are generated from m and the final computed values of *psum* and *pucp*, which are *sum* and *ucp*.
8. *meanacpf(m,sum,ucp,sfac)* $\rightarrow$ *mean* $\wedge$ *acp*. The final values of

psum and *pucp* are *sum* and *ucp*. They are used, along with *m*, to compute *mean* and *acp*.

9. *meanf(sum,m)* → *mean*. The mean is computed from *sum* and *m*.
10. *acpf(ucp,sfac,mean,m)* → *acp*. The adjusted cross products (*acp*) are computed from *ucp*, *sfac*, *m* and *mean*.
11. *vcvf(acp,m)* → *vcv*. The variance-covariance matrix is computed from *acp* and *m*.

C. Structure diagram. The structure diagram for *covar* is contained in Figure 2.4.

2.5 FUNCTIONS AND DETAILED DESIGN

Detailed designs provide more information about the data and functions in a general design and may introduce new, less abstract data and functions. They include details of the variables and structures that will be used and a general description of the control logic.

The following examples indicate the places in which functions occur in detailed designs. In each example, the design is divided into four parts. The first part contains information about data and data structures. The second part contains information about explicit functions. These are functions that

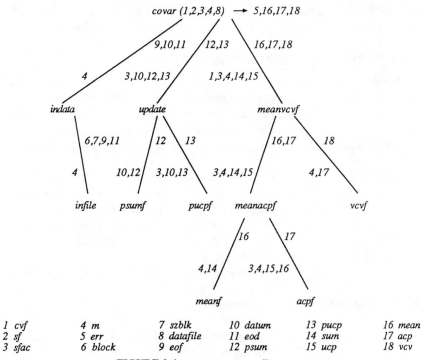

FIGURE 2.4. *covar* structure diagram.

are explicitly used in the detailed design and are referenced in the design's control logic description. The third part of the design is a *functional design language* (fdl) description of the program's control logic. The fdl descriptions are similar to *program design language* (pdl)[3] or pseudo-code descriptions. Recall that program design languages consist of intermixed comments and programming language control constructs. The fdl which is used in the following examples is a combination of functional and Algol-like notation. Unlike traditional program design languages, prose comments are not used to indicate undefined computations. Instead, functions are created which have the effect of such comments and are used in their place. The details of the fdl which is used are defined in Section 2.5.1.

The fourth part of each detailed design describes implicit functions. These are functions that do not occur directly in the detailed design fdl. In some cases they are functions which were documented in the general design or the requirements, but in the fdl they disappear and are implemented as parts of programs or distributed sections of code. Sometimes several implicit functions are intertwined together in the same code. An additional class of implicit functions in the fdl are the *programming functions*. These are functions that are introduced in order to translate the functional requirements and design into a programming language. They include, for example, loop counting functions or data access and storage functions. The implicit functions are not traditionally identified in a system builder's detailed design document, but they are critical to testing and analysis and should be included.

2.5.1   Functional Design Language (fdl)

A. Control constructs.

repeat until:	causes repetition of the code between the repeat until and the matching repeatend with a test at the end of the loop for loop termination.
repeat while:	the same as repeat until except the loop exit test is made at the beginning of the loop.
repeatend:	indicates the end of a loop.
if then else:	conventional conditional statement. Compound statements included in the scope of a then or else are denoted by suitable indentation and not by anything like a begin or end construct.
return( ):	used to return from a function. The value(s) of the variables in the parentheses are returned as the value of the function.

B. Function and subroutine definitions.

function( ):	denotes the beginning of a function definition. Input parameters are included in the parentheses. No information is returned in these calls by value parameters.

endfunction: denotes the end of a function definition.

subroutine( ):   like a conventional subroutine with call by refer-
                       ence parameters. Values can be both input to and
                       returned from the subroutine using the parame-
                       ters. Unlike functions, invocation of a subroutine
                       does not result in the return of a value for the sub-
                       routine as a whole.

endsubroutine: denotes the end of a subroutine definition.

C. Subroutine and function calls. This is done in the normal way using the
   name of a subroutine or function. Function calls can be treated like variables since they return a value for the function as a whole.

D. Assignment. This is indicated using a back arrow as in

$$bscore \leftarrow score$$

E. Data structures and variables. The principal goal in the fdl is to avoid
   forcing the designer to make decisions about functions and data before
   he is ready to make those decisions. For functions, this is easily achieved
   by allowing the use of functions and subroutines that have not yet been
   defined. For data, this is achieved in several ways.

   The fdl language contains ordinary untyped, undeclared variables
   which the user can create and use at any place in the program text. It also
   contains standard data structures (vectors, arrays, records, and lists) that
   can be used in the same way. The indexing notation for vectors and arrays is conventional. Parts of structured records can be accessed using
   the dot notation so that

$$rec1.dater.religion$$

denotes the *religion* part of the *dater* part of the record *rec1*.

   The most important distinction in the use of data structures and
   variables is that they can be created "on the fly," as needed, and do not
   have to be declared at the beginning of fdl functions.

   In addition to allowing the user to create and use standard variables
   and data structures, the fdl allows the designer to use functional notation
   to create and use incompletely defined, nonstandard data structures. Suppose that *clmessage* is a data object receiving a value in the assignment

$$clmessage \leftarrow getdt(clientid)$$

and it is not clear yet what the different kinds of data are that might or
should be returned by *getdt*, but it is known that the object should contain some information *info*, and it should also have a Boolean component
nocl that can be either unset (i.e., have value *nil*) or set to value *true*.
Then the user can simply assume this information to be available by
creating a function with the appropriate name which accesses the data object for the data, so that

$$nocl(clmessage)$$

refers to the *nocl* Boolean part of *clmessage*, and

$$info(clmessage)$$

refers to the information part. If the construct occurs on the right-hand side of an assignment, the value of the appropriate data in the data object is returned. If the construct occurs on the left-hand side of an assignment, the appropriate part of the data object is assigned a value.

If a function is listed as returning either compound or alternative types of data, then fdl functional notation can be used to access the appropriate kind of data. Suppose, for example, the construct

$$updt(clientinfo,dateinfo,bdate,bscore) \rightarrow bdate \wedge bscore$$

occurs in a listing of the functions in a system. Then the data object returned by *updt* will have a *bdate* part and a *bscore* part. Suppose *message* contains a data object returned by *updt*. Then these parts of the data object can be accessed using the functional notation

$$bdate(message) \quad \text{and} \quad bscore(message).$$

Suppose that the alternatives construct

$$getdt(clientid) \rightarrow clientinfo \vee nocl$$

occurs in a function definition, and that *message* contains data returned by *getdt*. Then the convention is used that

$$clientinfo(message)$$

either returns the *clientinfo* type of data in message, if that is the type of data that was returned by *getdt*, or returns *nil*, indicating that that is not the type of data returned. The *nocl* data is treated similarly.

2.5.2   Dating System Example

A. Data and data structures.
1. *daterequest*. This is stored on a unit record input device. It is a single integer *id* in the range [1, 9999].
2. *clientid*. The client who made the client request is identified internally by the number on the *daterequest*. It will be stored in a variable with the appropriate range.
3. *clientinfo*. The client information record contains the information described in the requirements. It can be stored in a data structure of the type *daterecord*, described in Figure 2.5.
4. *nocl*. A simple Boolean variable can be used to implement this flag.
5. *dateinfo*. Implemented using a *daterecord* data structure.

dater		
id	integer	$1 \leq id \leq 9999$
sex	character	1 byte
religion	character	10 bytes
occupation	character	12 bytes
politics	character	12 bytes
weight	integer	$1 \leq weight \leq 500$
height	integer	$1 \leq height \leq 100$
datee		
sex	character	1 byte
religion	character	10 bytes
occupation	character	12 bytes
politics	character	12 bytes
weight		
min	integer	$1 \leq min \leq 500$
max	integer	$1 \leq max \leq 500$
height		
min	integer	$1 \leq min \leq 100$
max	integer	$1 \leq max \leq 100$

FIGURE 2.5. *daterecord* data structure.

6. *bdate*. A date record implemented using a *daterecord* data structure.
7. *bscore*. Implemented by an integer variable capable of holding non-negative integers in the range [1,12].
8. *score*. An integer variable holding the same kind of data as *bscore*.
9. *better*. Either implicitly implemented as part of a conditional statement or with a Boolean variable.
10. *bestmatch*. The final value of *bdate*.
11. *report*. Line printer output consisting of a message "no data record for client found'' or the contents of *bestmatch*.
12. *datefile*. A sequential file with several supporting access routines, one of which simulates random access. Each record in the file is of the *daterecord* type.

B. Explicit functions. There are several new functions to consider in the detailed design as well as the details of general design functions.
1. *halfbliss(rec1,rec2)* $\rightarrow$ *nscore* where *rec1* and *rec2* can be either *clientinfo* or *dateinfo*. This function computes the "one way" match-score for two people, that is, how much the person represented by *rec2* "likes" the person represented by *rec1*. It will be implemented as a separate routine and is used by the function *blissf*.
2. *getdt(clientid)* $\rightarrow$ *nocl* $\vee$ *clientinfo*. This function accesses the *datefile* randomly on the basis of a client identification number and returns a message which will be either an error indicator or the record associated with the client id number.
3. *initializedtfile*. The *datefile* is initialized for sequential access.
4. *getnextdt* $\rightarrow$ *dateinfo*. It is assumed that the *datefile* has been initialized for sequential access and there is at least one more record to be read. This record is returned.

   5. *enddtfile* → true or false. If the last record in the *datefile* has been reached, the Boolean value *true* is returned. Otherwise, *false* is returned.
C. Fdl. Figures 2.6, 2.7, and 2.8 contain the functional design language specification for the *dater, blissf* and *halfbliss* functions.
D. Implicit functions.
   1. *bestdate*. This functional transformation occurs explicitly in the dataflow requirements but is implicit in the *dater* fdl. It is associated with the updating operations on lines 12–14 in the fdl, and the return of *bdate* on line 16.
   2. *getrequest*. This is explicit in the general design but is computed implicitly in *dater* as part of the function call mechanism.
   3. *initializebscore*. This detailed design function, used to initialize the data operated on by *updt* and *scrcompare*, is implicitly implemented in line 7.
   4. *updt*. The updating function in the general design is also implicit in lines 12–14 of the fdl.
   5. *scrcompare*. Also explicit in the general design, but implemented by part of a conditional statement in the fdl.
   6. Programming functions. The *dater* fdl implements implicit programming functions in each of the assignment statements. They correspond to the functions of accessing data, as on the right-hand side of an assignment, and storing data, as on the left-hand side of an assignment. In addition, in the *dater* fdl, there are two Boolean decision functions corresponding to the two if-then statements. Finally, there is a repeat-while function. It determines how many times to repeat the code in the repeat-endrepeat code section. In this case the code is to be repeated for all *daterecord* records in *datefile* so that

```
function dater(daterequest)                              1
    clientid ← id(daterequest)                           2
    clmessage ← getdt(clientid)                          3
    if nocl(clmessage) ≠ nil                             4
        then return ("error: no such daterclient")       5
    clientinfo ← info(clmessage)                         6
    bscore ← 0                                           7
    initializedtfile                                     8
    repeat while not (enddtfile)                         9
        dateinfo ← getnextdt                             10
        score ← blissf(clientinfo,dateinfo)             11
        if score > bscore                               12
            then bscore ← score                         13
                 bdate ← dateinfo                       14
    endrepeat                                            15
    return(bdate)                                        16
endfunction                                              17
```

FIGURE 2.6. Fdl for *dater* function.

```
function blissf(clientinfo,dateinfo)
     return(halfbliss(clientinfo,dateinfo) + halfbliss(dateinfo,clientinfo))
endfunction
```

FIGURE 2.7. Fdl for *blissf* function.

the repeat function implicitly calculates the number of such records in the database.

There are similar programming functions in the *blissf* and *halfbliss* pseudo-code.

2.5.3 *covar* Statistics Example

A. Data and data structures.
  1. *cvf*. Implemented with a single Boolean variable.
  2. *sf*. Implemented with a single Boolean variable.
  3. *sfac*. This is implemented with a floating-point vector of length n. Depending on *sf*, it is either set before entry to the routine or the first set of observations from *datefile* is copied into it.
  4. *m*. A single integer variable.
  5. *err*. Implemented using a string variable or character vector for storing error messages.
  6. *block*. Each input block of variable observations $x(k,i,j)$, $1 \leq i \leq szblk(k)$, $1 \leq j \leq n$, is stored in the m by n array $temp(i,j)$, $1 \leq i \leq mxblk$, $1 \leq j \leq n$. m is the total number of observations. If $mxblk$ divides evenly into m, then each block of observations will fill *temp* entirely. Otherwise, the last block will contain less than $mxblk$ observations and, more specifically, *temp* will contain $remainder(m/mxblk)$ new entries. The rest of *temp*, for this last small block, will be indeterminate. The number of *blocks* will be either $m/mxblk$ or $m/mxblk + 1$, depending on whether $mxblk$ divides evenly into m or not.

```
function halfbliss(rec1,rec2)
     score ← 0
     if rec1.dater.sex = rec2.datee.sex then score ← score + 1
     if rec1.dater.religion = rec2.datee.religion then score ← score + 1
     if rec1.dater.occupation = rec2.datee.occupation then score ← score + 1
     if rec1.dater.politics = rec2.datee.politics then score ← score + 1
     if rec2.datee.weight.min ≤ rec1.dater.weight ≤ rec2.datee.weight.max
          then score ← score + 1
     if rec2.datee.height.min ≤ rec1.dater.height ≤ rec2.datee.height.max
          then score ← score + 1
     return (score)
endfunction
```

FIGURE 2.8. Fdl for *halfbliss* function.

7. *datafile*. The input file. If the target language is Fortran, it may be a logical device number.
8. *eof*. This is implementation dependent. It can be implemented by a Boolean variable set by the input function when there are no more record blocks to be read.
9. *datum* is a row of values in the array *temp*.
10. *eod*. This will not be explicitly implemented in the fdl or program.
11. *psum*. The partial sum values will be stored in the floating-point vector *mean(i)*, $1 \leq i \leq m$. After the processing of an intermediate number of blocks of observations, *mean(i)*, $1 \leq i \leq n$, will contain the sums of the observations seen so far.
12. *pucp*. The partial unadjusted cross products will be stored in the floating point array *vcv(i,j)*, $1 \leq i \leq m$, $1 \leq j \leq n$. After the processing of an intermediate number of blocks of observations, *vcv(i,j)* will contain the cross products for variables *i* and *j* for the observations seen so far.
13. *sum*. The complete sums of variable observations will be stored in *mean(i)*, $1 \leq i \leq m$.
14. *ucp*. The unadjusted cross products will also be stored in *vcv(i,j)*, $1 \leq i \leq m$, $1 \leq j \leq n$.
15. *mean*. The mean data will be in *mean(i)*, $1 \leq i \leq m$.
16. *acp*. The adjusted cross products will also be stored in the array *vcv(i,j)*, $1 \leq i \leq m$, $1 \leq j \leq n$.
17. *vcv*. If the flag *cvf* indicates it, the variance-covariance values for the observations will be the final values in the array *vcv(i,j)*, $1 \leq i \leq m$, $1 \leq j \leq n$.

B. Explicit functions.
1. *valinf(n,m,mxblk)* → true $\bigvee$ false. The ranges of values of input parameters can be checked to confirm that

$$n \geq 1, \qquad m \geq 2, \qquad \text{and} \qquad m \geq mxblk.$$

2. *szblkf(k,m,mx blk)* → *szblk(k)*. This function calculates the number of observations in a block. It is computed by:

    if $k <$ *numblksf(m,mxblk)*
        then *szblk(k)* = *mxblk*
        else if *remainder(m,mxblk)* = 0
            then *szblk(k)* = *mxblk*
            else *szblk(k)* = *remainder(m,mxblk)*

where *numblksf(m,mxblk)* calculates the number of blocks of data of size *mxblk* that a file of size *m* will be divided up into.
3. *initializearrays(mean,vcv)*. Sets the values of the arrays to 0.
4. *getablockofdata(f,temp,mxb lk,m,k,szblk,eof)*. This function reads in data from the file identified by *f* and stores it in *temp*. It updates *k*,

the total number of records so far, and reading is halted if $k = m$, the total number of records to be used. *szblk* indicates the number of records read into the block. The variable *eof* is set to true if an end-of-file condition occurred before m records were read.

5. *getscalingfactorsfromobservations(temp,sfac)*. Copies the first set of observations in *temp* into the scaling factors vector, *sfac*.
6. *updatepsum(temp,i,mean)*. Uses the ith set of observations in *temp* to update the partial sum stored in *mean*.
7. *updatepucp(temp,i,vcv)*. Uses the ith set of observations in *temp* to update the partial unadjusted cross products stored in *vcv*.
8. *constructmeanfromsum(mean,m)*. Divides the sums stored in *mean* by m in order to turn them into means.
9. *transformucptoacp(vcv,mean,sfac,m)*. Adjusts the unadjusted cross products in *vcv* for the mean, turning them into adjusted cross products.
10. *transformacptovcv(vcv,m)*. Changes the adjusted cross products to variance-covariance data by dividing by $(m - 1)$.

C. Fdl. Figure 2.9 contains the fdl for *covar*. In this example subroutines rather than functions are used.
D. Implicit functions.
1. *scalingfactors*. Depending on the value of *sf*, *covar* will leave the input values of *sfac* unchanged or will compute new values using the fdl function *getscalingfactorsfromobservations*. This implicit function is implemented in *covar* by lines 6 and 7 in the fdl.
2. *indata*. This is implemented using the repeat loop beginning on line 11, which sets i to point to the row in *temp* to access, and the refer-

```
subroutine covar(cvf,sf,sfac,m,n,mxblk,temp,f,mean,vcv,err)      1
    if valinf(n,m,mxblk) = false then err ← "bad data"          2
                    return                                       3
    initializearrays(mean,vcv)                                   4
    k ← 0; eof ← false                                           5
    getablockofdata(f,temp,mxblk,m,k,szblk,eof)                  6
    if sf = 1 then getscalingfactorsfromobservations(temp,sfac)  7
    repeat while k < m                                           8
        if eof = true then err ← "missing observations"          9
                    return                                      10
        repeat for i = 1 to szblk                               11
            updatepsum(temp,i,mean)                             12
            updatepucp(temp,i,vcv)                              13
        endrepeat                                               14
        getablockofdata(f,temp,mxblk,m,k,szblk,eof)             15
    endrepeat                                                   16
    constructmeanfromsum(mean,m)                                17
    transformucptoacp(vcv,mean,sfac,m)                          18
    if cvf = 1 then transformacptovcv(vcv,m)                    19
endsubroutine                                                   20
```

FIGURE 2.9. Fdl for *covar* program.

ences to this row that will occur inside *updatesum* and *updatepucp*. The repeat loop control mechanism also implicitly implements the part of *indata* which causes the invocation of *getablockofdata* when a new set of observations is to be read in.

3. *update*. This function in the general design is almost explicit in the two fdl functions *updatesum* and *updatepucp*.

4. *numblks(m,mxblk)*. The fdl can be thought of as implicitly calculating how many blocks of data are read in. This is described by the expression

$$\lceil m/mxblk \rceil$$

where $\lceil \ \rceil$ denotes least integer greater than or equal to.

5. *symindxf(i,j)*. In order to conserve storage, the symmetric matrix *vcv( )* will be stored as a vector. It is accessed using the indexing function computed by the formula:

$$i * (i - 1)/2 + j$$

where it is assumed that $i \leq j$. This function is not implicit like the others but is not contained in the *covar* fdl because it is at a lower level of detail than the fdl.

The fdl for *covar* contains the same kind of programming functions as found in the *dater* fdl.

2.6   PROGRAM FUNCTIONS

The programs for the dating system and the *covar* example will not be given here since no new information about function identification can be added to that which was given in the examples. For both examples, the functions are the same for programs as they are for fdl's.

2.7   FUNCTIONS AND COMMENTS

Most of the functions in the examples given could be easily identified, and their meanings derived, from the function names. It is sometimes desirable in fdl program descriptions, or in program code, to include comments to help identify functions. There are two kinds of common situations. The first is to identify implicit functions, and the second is to provide more detail about particular functions than is present in the function name. Comments can also be used for other testing purposes, some of which are described in later chapters.

Figure 2.10 reproduces Figure 2.6 with comments embedded which identify several implicit functions and which elaborate on several explicit functions. It is important to note that these comments do not stand for miss-

```
function dater(daterequest)
    clientid ← id(daterequest)
    clmessage ← getdt(clientid)
    if nocl(clmessage) ≠ nil {see if any client data returned by getdt}
        then return ("error: no such client")
    clientinfo ← info(clmessage) {get client data returned by getdt}
    bscore ← 0 {initialize bscore}
    initializedtfile
    repeat while not (enddtfile)
        dateinfo ← getnextdt
        score ← blissf(clientinfo,dateinfo)
        if score > bscore        {scrcompare}
            then {updt}
                bscore ← score
                bdate ← dateinfo
    endrepeat
    return(bdate)
endfunction
```

FIGURE 2.10. Comments and implicit functions.

ing data or functions, as is the case for conventional pseudo-code, but are explanations of computations already included in the fdl.

2.8 SUMMARY

Two very different examples were presented to illustrate how functions arise, and their central importance, in the software development process. For both examples, the requirements and general and detailed designs were given. In the first, a data processing example, there was a smooth flow of increasing detail from one development product to the next. The data-flow requirements contained a set of abstract data-flow transformation functions. The general design involved general functional modules in a structure diagram. The detailed design introduced an additional, detailed submodule function. In the other example, the formal requirements specifications were given for the scientific program *covar*. As in the first example, there was a smooth flow of increasingly detailed functions, from the specifications through the general design to the detailed design.

In both examples a particular requirements and design methodology was used. Structured Analysis was used for requirements and Structured Design for general design. The central role of functions in other types of requirements and design methods, such as Jackson design,[4,5] can also be demonstrated.

One of the important concepts in the two examples is the notion of an *implicit function*. This is a function which is not explicit in the detailed design or implementation of a program in the sense that it is not encapsulated in a function or subroutine definition. In some cases a function corresponds to discontiguous sections of code and in other cases it is intertwined with the code for several other functions. Some implicit functions are explicit in the general design. Others are quantities which are only indirectly computed by a program, and whose values are not used in any intermediate computation or any program output. Examples of implicit functions include the *scaling-factors* function in *covar*. This function occurs as a result of the combined effects of a conditional test on a variable *sf* and a call to the routine *getscalingfactorsfromobservations*.

Both fdl designs and programs also contain *programming functions* which are used to manage program control flow and to cause the transfer of data from one location to another. Examples include loop control functions for counting the number of times a loop has been traversed, and assignment and retrieval functions for saving and accessing data. The repeat-loop termination condition "while $k < m$" in the *covar* fdl, for example, is a loop control programming function. It calculates whether or not to exit from a loop.

Comments can be used to identify the presence of implicit functions or to provide additional detail about explicit functions.

EXERCISES

2.1. In *forward dependency analysis,* the functions belonging to one set of software documents are "traced forward" to a more refined set to confirm that every function in the first set is supported by one or more functions in the second set. *Backwards dependency analysis* can be used to confirm that each function in the more refined set is needed to implement at least one function in the original, less refined set. Construct tables showing the forwards and backwards dependencies between the requirements and general design functions for the dating system example. Determine if there are any unsupported requirements functions or unneeded design functions.

2.2. Repeat Exercise 2.1 for the general and detailed design functions in the dating example.

2.3. Repeat Exercises 2.1 and 2.2 and for the *covar* requirements, general design, and detailed design functions.

2.4. Construct a general and a detailed design for the following problem. Identify all explicit and implicit functions introduced during the design process.

"The program is to read text from a character file and to print it out, one line at a time. Each line is to contain 132 characters, including blanks. The program is to both left and right justify the text so that there are no blanks at the left- and right-hand ends of lines except the first and possibly the last lines of paragraphs. It does this by inserting extra blanks in between words."

"The text consists of words separated by one or more blanks and a special word pp which denotes the end of one paragraph and the beginning of another. The first line of each paragraph should be indented by five spaces and should be right justified. The last line of each paragraph should be left justified."

2.5. Construct a systematic approach to the recognition of functions for an alternative design methodology such as the Jackson design method.[4,5]

REFERENCES

1. T. DeMarco, *Structured Analysis and System Specification,* Yourdon Press, N.Y., 1978.
2. E. Yourdon and L. Constantine, *Structured Design,* Prentice-Hall, Englewood Cliffs, N.J., 1979.
3. S. H. Caine and K. E. Gordon, PDL—A tool for software design, *Proceedings National Computer Conference,* vol. 44, 1975.
4. M. A. Jackson, *Principles of Program Design,* Academic Press, London, 1975.
5. M. A. Jackson, *System Development*, Prentice-Hall, London, 1983.

CHAPTER
3

STATES
AND
TYPES

3.1 SOFTWARE DEVELOPMENT—
STATES AND TYPES

Chapter 2 described the central role of functions in all stages of the software development process. Functions occur as basic building blocks in requirements documents and in general and detailed designs. They can be either explicit or implicit. This chapter describes the complementary central roles of data types and data states. They too are basic building blocks at all levels of software development and must be taken into account during testing and analysis.

3.2 DATA TYPES AND ABSTRACT
DATA STRUCTURES

In Chapter 2 types were introduced as parts of function definitions. Functions transform objects of one type into objects of other types. Informally, *types* are sets of objects which are all of the same kind. Two objects are of the same kind if they have the same kinds of properties and the same kinds of operations can be performed on them. Common data types are integers, strings of characters, and floating-point numbers. The common operations that can be performed on integers, for example, are *integer add, subtract, multiply,* and *divide*. Common Boolean properties include *positive* and *negative*.

It is often the case that there are different kinds of data that look the same but mean something quite different. In the *covar* example, both the *sum* and the *mean* for variable observations are floating-point numbers, and in fact, both are stored in the same variable, but they mean something quite different. These kinds of types will be called *flavors*.

Types may also be sets of complex structured objects, such as arrays, stacks, lists, and files. One approach to characterizing such types is in terms of axioms defining their storage and retrieval operators.[1] The classic example is that of a stack. Figure 3.1 contains an axiomatic definition for a stack of integers.

The first line in the definition identifies the type being defined. The second identifies a type which is already assumed to be defined and whose properties and operators may be used in the new definition. The third section shows the input and output types of each operator and the fourth section shows the axioms defining the operators. The definition is incomplete since it does not define what happens when an attempt is made to *pop* an empty stack.

It is possible in an abstract data type definition to simultaneously define several types of data with axioms that involve the combined use of their operators. This idea has been extended to allow complete programs to be written as abstract data type definitions, but usually this is not useful and only results in program-like structures that are difficult to understand.

3.3 VARIABLES, DATA STRUCTURES, AND STATES

Different programming languages contain different kinds of built-in data types and data structures. The programmer has to map the types of the problem on to the data structures available in the language. The variables and data structures in a program can be looked at in two ways. One way is as denoting objects of a certain type and the other way is as storage structures for holding objects of the appropriate type. The second point of view will be adopted. Note that it is not unusual for a variable to be used for several different types of data, or at least different flavors. In the *covar* example the array *vcv* is used at different times to hold unadjusted cross products, cross products, and variance-covariances.

type:	*integerstack*
uses:	*integers*
operators:	*push(integer,integerstack)* $\rightarrow$ *integerstack*
	pop(integerstack) $\rightarrow$ *integerstack*
	top(integerstack) $\rightarrow$ *integer*
axioms:	*pop(push(x,s))* $\rightarrow$ *s*
	top(push(x,s)) $\rightarrow$ *x*

FIGURE 3.1. Axioms for stack of integers.

Data structures are considered to be in different states depending on the type of data they contain or on properties of the data. The *vcv* array, for example, can be in the state {*vcv* is *unadjustedcrossproducts*} when it contains that type of data. Some states are *history states*, in the sense that they denote what has been done to the data in a data structure. Suppose, for example, it is necessary to check if the account number in a new record just read into a data structure is the same as the old account number. Then before the check and after the new record has been read in, the record data structure is in the state *unchecked*. Afterwards it is in the *checked* state. These two kinds of data are flavors of the account number type of data.

In general, the state of a system or program is associated with the contents of all of its variables and data structures. *State assertions* describe relationships between data. State assertions and functions have a complementary relationship. Functions transform one program state into another and a program can be described in terms of either the sequences of state transforming computations it performs or the sequences of states it goes through during its sequences of computations.

3.4 TYPES AND REQUIREMENTS

At the requirements level of system description, types of data are used rather than states of variables and data structures since few, if any, variables or data structures will have been defined. The system is described as transforming one kind of data into another.

3.4.1 Dating System Example

Figure 3.2 reproduces the data-flow diagram for the requirements for the dating system. Only the data-flow arcs have been labeled. Each of the data-flow names can be interpreted as a data type, and the program requirements as an interconnected system of transformations of one type of data into another. Additional information about the data types occurs in the data dictionary for the system, included in Chapter 2 in Figure 2.2. The importance of data types in the construction of the system is clear in this example.

3.4.2 *covar* Statistics Program Example

The role of types is not as pronounced in the formal specifications for the *covar* example as for the dating system, since there is no modeling of internal type transformations. But it is still possible to view the program entirely in terms of its input and output types. Figure 3.3 contains a simple data type transformation diagram which depicts *covar* as a type transformer. Descriptive names have been used for the data types. The data names used in the specification are included in parentheses after the data type names.

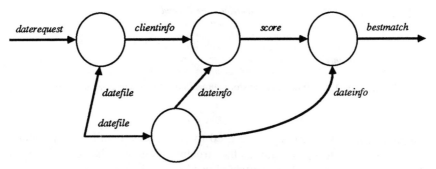

FIGURE 3.2.   Dating system data type transformations.

3.5   TYPES AND GENERAL DESIGN

General designs, like requirements, emphasize data types rather than states of variables and data structures. The role of types as a basic concept in the construction of general designs can be seen in both the dating and *covar* examples. In the structured designs for these examples, the structure diagrams emphasized their hierarchical functional structure. Data couples were used to illustrate the data flow between the functions. The data couples can be interpreted as data types and the structure diagram as a type transformer like a data-flow diagram. In the Structured Analysis/Structured Design approach to system construction, this correspondence is carried even further, with actual rules for converting a data-flow diagram into a hierarchical structure diagram.[2]

3.5.1   Dating System Example

Figure 3.4 contains a list of the data types in the structured design for the dating system and shows the implied type transformations in the structure

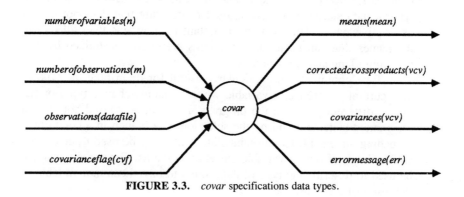

FIGURE 3.3.   *covar* specifications data types.

$$daterequest \rightarrow clientid$$
$$clientid \rightarrow clientinfo \lor nocl$$
$$clientinfo \land dateinfo \rightarrow score$$
$$score \land bscore \land bdate \rightarrow better$$
$$dateinfo \land bscore \land bdate \land better \rightarrow bscore \land bdate$$
$$bscore \land bdate \rightarrow bestmatch$$

FIGURE 3.4. Types and transformations in dating system general design.

diagram. This information can be used to construct a data-flow representation at the same level of detail as the structure diagram. The general design data flow for the example is contained in Figure 3.5.

3.5.2 *covar* Statistics Program Example

The increased data information in the general design for *covar* consists of more data types and type transformations. The general design data types, and the type transformations implicit in the structure diagram for *covar*, are listed in Figure 3.6. A data-flow representation like that for the dating system general design could also be constructed. In both this and the dating system example, the data types are as basic to the understanding and construction of the program as are the functions described in Chapter 2.

3.6 STATES, TYPES, AND DETAILED DESIGN

The data types and system states that occur in a detailed design can be documented using fdl comments. Several different kinds of comments can be identified.

1. Type comments. These can be used to describe the type of data currently stored in a variable or data structure, and are of the form {*varname* is *type*}. Type comments like this can be used for describing the type of data stored in a variable or data structure that does not have a descriptive name. This is more important in programs than fdl's since the names that can be used in programs are often constrained by programming language conventions.

   Type comments are particularly useful for describing the type of data currently stored in a variable whose contents change type, or flavor, at different points in the program. This can be caused both by an assignment statement and by the selection of a branch in a conditional branching statement. Conditional statements may be used to determine which flavor of data a variable currently contains. Type comments can be used to describe the type of data found to have been in a variable as the result of a conditional test.

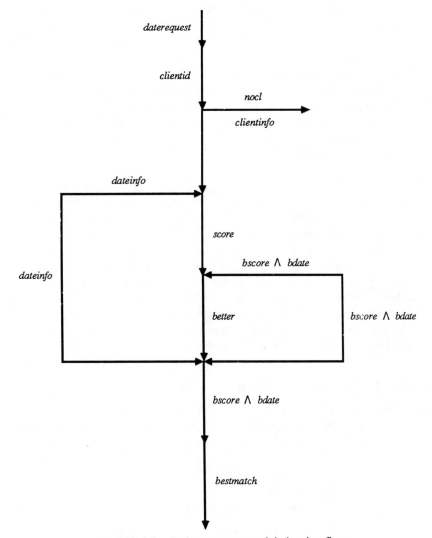

FIGURE 3.5. Dating system general design data flow.

$$m \rightarrow eof \vee eod \vee (block \wedge szblk)$$
$$block \rightarrow datum$$
$$sfac \wedge datum \wedge psum \wedge pucp \rightarrow psum \wedge pucp$$
$$datum \wedge psum \rightarrow psum$$
$$datum \wedge pucp \rightarrow pucp$$
$$sfac \wedge m \wedge sum \wedge acp \rightarrow mean \wedge (acp \vee vcv)$$
$$sfac \wedge m \wedge sum \wedge ucp \rightarrow mean \wedge acp$$
$$m \wedge mean \wedge acp \rightarrow vcv$$
$$m \wedge sum \rightarrow mean$$
$$sfac \wedge m \wedge ucp \wedge mean \rightarrow acp$$

FIGURE 3.6. Types and transformations in *covar* general design.

2. Program states. These may be used to describe relationships between program variables and data structures. A formal language of relationships and properties may be used to allow automated analysis of program states.

3. Explanation comments. These are used to paraphrase a computation which has occurred in a program or to provide a fuller description of the properties of data stored in a variable than can be included in its name. These are more informal than the first two kinds of comments and provide explanations about a type of data rather than declare what type is stored in a variable.

The classes of comments just described are informal and a comment could be interpreted as belonging to more than one class. Comments about the outcome of a conditional statement, for example, might be interpreted as either type or explanation comments. If the variable and data structure names in a program or fdl are carefully chosen, then the program can be described as being self-documenting. This means that the names describe the types of data stored in variables so that type comments are not necessary. In addition to state and type comments, recall that a program or fdl may contain operator comments that associate a function or operator name with part of the code. Additional kinds of comments, which are associated with structural analysis of fdl's, are described in Chapter 6.

3.6.1 Dating System Example

The first version of the commented *dater* fdl, in Figure 3.7, contains the type comments necessary to identify the types of data stored in the fdl variables and data structures. The *dater* fdl is almost entirely self-documenting

```
function dater(daterequest)
    clientid ← id(daterequest)
    clmessage ← getdt(clientid)
    if nocl(clmessage) ≠ nil
        then return("error: no such daterclient")
    clientinfo ← info(clmessage)
    bscore ← 0
    initializedtfile
    repeat while not (enddtfile)
        dateinfo← getnextdt
        score ← blissf(clientinfo,dateinfo)
        if score > bscore
            then bscore ← score
                bdate ← dateinfo
    endrepeat
    {bdate is bestmatch}
    return(bdate)
endfunction
```

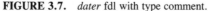

FIGURE 3.7.   *dater* fdl with type comment.

with the exception of a flavor change in a variable. The comment is needed at the point where the data stored in *bdate* (bestdate) changes from *bdate* data to *bestmatch* data. This flavor change occurs at the end of the repeat loop in the fdl.

The second version of *dater*, in Figure 3.8, contains two explanation comments and an operator comment. The operator comment identifies the initialization operation for *bscore*. In general, the decision to include which comments in a program will be based on the purpose of the comments. If it is for the purpose of automated program analysis, then only certain special kinds might be used.

3.6.2 *covar* Statistics Program Example

The first commented fdl for *covar* is in Figure 3.9 and contains type comments describing the different flavors of data that are stored in the variables and data structures. There are more of these in *covar* than in *dater* for two reasons. The first is that the use of variables and data structures in *covar* is closer to that of a program in the sense that they are reused for different data whenever possible. The second is that the variable and data structure names in *covar* are not self-documenting and type comments are necessary to identify the type(s) of data they will contain.

Figure 3.10 contains the second commented version of *covar*. In this case the fdl has been commented with a complete set of formal assertions that describe the relationships between the program's variables and data structures at different places in the program. These are the kinds of comments needed to construct formal proofs of correctness. Several notational

```
function dater(daterequest)
    clientid ← id(daterequest)
    clmessage ← getdt(clientid)
    if nocl(clmessage) ≠ nil
        then {client with id clientid is not in database}
            return("error: no such daterclient")
    {information for client with id clientid is in database}
    clientinfo ← info(clmessage)
    bscore ← 0 {initialize bscore}
    initializedtfile
    repeat while not(enddtfile)
        dateinfo ← getnextdt
        score ← blissf(clientinfo,dateinfo)
        if score > bscore
            then {score for new potential date better}
                {than previous bestscore}
                bscore ← score
                bdate ← dateinfo
    endrepeat
    return(bdate)
endfunction
```

FIGURE 3.8   *dater* fdl with explanation comments.

subroutine *covar(cvf,sf,sfac,m,n,mxblk,temp,f,mean,vcv,err)*
{*cvf is covariance flag; m is numberofobservations; sf is scaling flag; sfac is scalingfactors*}
    if *valinf(n,m,mxblk)* = false then *err* ← *"bad data"*
                            return
initializearrays(mean,vcv)
k ← 0; *eof* ← false
getablockofdata(f,temp,mxblk,m,k,szblk,eof) {*temp is observations*}
if *sf* = 1 then *getscalingfactorsfromobservations(temp,sfac)* {*sfac is scalingfactors*}
repeat while $k < m$
    if *eof* = true then *err* ← *"missing observations"*
                return
    repeat for i = 1 to *szblk*
        updatepsum(temp,i,mean) {*mean is sum*}
        updatepucp(temp,i,vcv) {*vcv is unadjustedcrossproducts*}
    endrepeat
    getablockofdata(f,temp,mxblk,m,k,szblk,eof)
endrepeat
constructmeanfromsum(mean,m) {*mean is mean*}
transformucptoacp(vcv,mean,sfac,m) {*vcv is adjustedcrossproducts*}
    if *cvf* = 1 then *transformacptovcv(vcv,m)* {*vcv is variancecovariance*}
endsubroutine

FIGURE 3.9.   *covar* fdl with type comments.

subroutine *covar(cvf,sf,sfac,m,n,mxblk,temp,f,mean,vcv,err)*
    if *valinf(n,m,mxblk)* = false then {$n < 1$ or $m < 2$ or $m < mxblk$}
                        err ← *"bad data"*
                        return
{$n \geq 1$ and $m \geq 2$ and $m \geq mxblk$}
initializearrays(mean,vcv)
{*mean(i)* = 0, $1 \leq i \leq n$; *vcv(i,j)* = 0, $1 \leq i \leq n$, $1 \leq j \leq n$}
k ← 0; *eof* ← false
getablockofdata(f,temp,mxblk,m,k,szblk,eof)
{{*eof* = true and *length(f)* $< m$} or
    {*eof* $\neq$ true and *temp(i,j)* = *record(f,i,j)*, $1 \leq i \leq mxblk$, $1 \leq j \leq n$, and
    szblk = k = *mxblk*}}
if *sf* = 1 then *getscalingfactorsfromobservations(temp,sfac)*
                {*sfac(j)* = *temp(i,j)*, $1 \leq j \leq n$}
repeat while $k < m$
    if *eof* = true then {*length(f)* $< m$}
                    err ← *"missing observations"*
                    return
{$k < m$ and $k < length(f)$}
repeat for i = 1 to *szblk*
    updatepsum(temp,i,mean)
    {*mean(j)* = *mean(j)'* + *temp(i,j)*, $1 \leq j \leq n$}
    updatepucp(temp,i,vcv)
    {*vcv(h,j)* = *vcv(h,j)'*
           + (*temp(i,j)* − *sfac(j)*) ∗ (*temp(i,h)* − *sfac(h)*)}
endrepeat

$$\{mean(j) = \sum_{i=1}^{k} record(f,i,j), \ 1 \leq j \leq n \ \text{and}$$

$$vcv(h,j) = \sum_{i=1}^{k} (record(f,i,j) - sfac(j)) \ast$$

$$(record(f,i,h) - sfac(h)), \ 1 \leq j \leq n, \ 1 \leq h \leq n\}$$

FIGURE 3.10.   Formal *covar* fdl states.

$getablockofdata(f,temp,mxblk,m,k,szblk,eof)$
$\{\{eof = false$ and $length(f) < m\}$ or
$\quad\{eof \neq false$ and $temp(i,j) = record(f,i + k',j),\ 1 \leq i \leq szblk,\ 1 \leq j \leq n\}\}$
$\quad\{$if $k < length(f)$ then $szblk = mxblk$
$\qquad\qquad\qquad\qquad$ else $szblk = remainder(length(f)/mxblk)\}$
$\{k = k' + szblk\}$
endrepeat

$$\{mean(j) = \sum_{i=1}^{m} record(f,i,j),\ 1 \leq j \leq n\}$$

$$\{vcv(h,j) = \sum_{i=1}^{m} (record(f,i,j) - sfac(j)) *$$

$$(record(f,i,h) - sfac(h)),\ 1 \leq j \leq n,\ 1 \leq h \leq n\}$$
$constructmeanfromsum(mean,m)$
$\{mean(j) = mean(j)'/m,\ 1 \leq j \leq n\}$
$transformucptoacp(vcv,mean,sfac,m)$
$\{vcv(h,j) = vcv(h,j)' - m * (mean(h) - sfac(h))$
$\qquad\qquad\qquad * (mean(j) - sfac(j)),\ 1 \leq h \leq n,\ 1 \leq j \leq n\}$
if $cvf = 1$ then $transformacptovcv(vcv,m)$
$\qquad\qquad\quad \{vcv(h,j) = vcv(h,j)'/(m - 1),\ 1 \leq h \leq n,\ 1 \leq j \leq n\}$

$$\{mean(j) = \sum_{i=1}^{m} record(f,i,j)/m,\ 1 \leq j \leq n\}$$

$\{$if $cvf = 1$ then $transformacptovcv(vcv,m)$

$$\{vcv(h,j) = (\sum_{i=1}^{m} (record(f,i,j) - sfac(j)) *$$

$$(record(f,i,h) - sfac(h)))/(m - 1),\ 1 \leq j \leq n,\ 1 \leq h \leq n\}$$

else $\{vcv(h,j) = \sum_{i=1}^{m} (record(f,i,j) - sfac(j)) *$

$$(record(f,i,h) - sfac(h)),\ 1 \leq j \leq n,\ 1 \leq h \leq n\}\}$$

endsubroutine

FIGURE 3.10. *(continued)*

conventions have been used. The function $record(f,i,j)$ refers to the jth field in record i of file f. These are the variable observations. The function $length(f)$ gives the number of records in f. The prime notation, as in $mean(j)'$, refers to the old value stored in $mean(j)$, as opposed to the new value now being put into $mean(j)$ in the associated assignment statement.

3.7 SUMMARY

The basic conceptual units in system design and construction are functions and types. They occur at all levels of abstraction in the description of a system or program. They have a complementary relationship in that functions can be described as state or type transformers.

Types are sets of data that correspond intuitively to the different kinds of data that are operated on and computed by a program. They can be simple, unstructured objects that can be stored in ordinary variables or complex, compound objects requiring the use of data structures. States are associated with variables and data structures in programs and fdl representations. Variables and data structures can be in different states depending on the types of data they contain. State descriptions can be used to provide explanations about computations and conditional branches, and may also describe global relationships between the data stored in different variables or data structures.

In program requirements and general designs it is types rather than states that are important. They describe the types of data that are input to, manipulated by, and output from a program or system. In detailed designs and programs, data is discussed in terms of the variables and data structures used to store it, and states become more important.

Program and fdl comments can be used to describe variable and data structure states. They can be used to identify the type of data currently stored in a variable, give formal state characterizations like those used in proofs of correctness, and provide explanations about computations or data types.

EXERCISES

3.1. Construct a data-type transformation (i.e., data-flow) diagram for the *covar* program general design, similar to that in Figure 3.5 for the dating system.

3.2. Identify the types and states in the software development documents generated by the exercise of Chapter 2, and construct a data-type transformation diagram.

3.3. One way of avoiding the need for type comments in fdl's is to require that separate variables be present for all types and not to allow one variable to hold more than one type of data. In the case where computations are being done on the data stored in a variable that causes an eventual change in type, the moment the change occurs the data must be moved to a new variable of the new type. Alter the fdl for *covar* in Figure 3.8 to include new variables so that they contain only one type of data.

3.4. The types of data stored in the variables on the right-hand side of an assignment statement are transformed into the type of data associated with the left-hand variable whenever the assignment is executed. Identify all such data transformations which occur in the *dater* fdl in Figure 3.7.

3.5. Repeat Exercise 3.4 using the *covar* fdl in Figure 3.9.

3.6. Compare the type transformations in Exercise 3.4 with the transformations that occur in the design data-flow diagrams for *dater* in Figure 3.5.

3.7. Repeat Exercise 3.6 using the data-flow diagram generated in Exercise 3.1.

3.8. Besides assignment statements, what are some of the other constructs in a program which result in the transformation of one kind of data into another?

3.9. Classification of data types occurs when a conditional statement tests the data stored in a variable, and on the basis of the test it is established that a certain subtype of data is present in the variable. In this case a more general kind of data is being "transformed" into a less general kind using the test. Analyze the fdl for *dater* in Figure 3.7 and identify all classificatory type transformations.

3.1 . Repeat Exercise 3.9 for the *covar* fdl in Figure 3.9.

REFERENCES

1. T. A. Goguen, J. W. Thatcher, and F. G. Wagner, Abstract data types as initial algebras and the correctness of data representations, in *Current Trends in Programming Methodology*, 4, R. Yeh (Ed.), Prentice-Hall, Englewood Cliffs, N.J., 1978, pp. 180–199.
2. E. Yourdon and L. Constantine, *Structured Design*, Prentice-Hall, Englewood Cliffs, N.J., 1979.

CHAPTER
4

THEORETICAL FOUNDATIONS

4.1 THEORY OF TESTING AND ANALYSIS

The previous chapters were relatively informal. No attempt was made to construct formal definitions for the concepts used or to formally prove observations about functions and types of data in programs. This chapter is significantly different. It introduces a variety of mathematical concepts and indicates how they can be used to prove properties of functional testing and analysis methods.

The first theoretical topic concerns the impossibility of devising a practical, systematic procedure for selecting test data which can be used to prove correctness. This is followed by a discussion of how functional testing and analysis avoids this problem. The use of a statistical approach to testing is then described. The sections following this prove a variety of theorems about arithmetic equations and inequalities. Arithmetic and Boolean algebra can be used to explain many important things about testing such as why, for example, testing at extremal values is effective. The algebraic results are used later in the discussion of functional testing in Chapter 5. Finally, some graph theory theorems are presented which can be used to design functional program analysis methods which depend on the traversal of program paths.

The theoretical material in this chapter is considerably more difficult than the other material, and the chapter can be viewed as a reference source. It is possible to skip most of the theoretical material in Sections 4.4 through

4.8, referring back to them only as necessary. In the following chapters, the theoretical material needed to support the use of particular testing and analysis methods is referenced, and the appropriate sections of Chapter 4 can be examined as needed. The exception to this is Section 4.3, which describes the basic concepts of the functional testing and analysis approach used in the book. It should be read before going on to the following chapters.

4.2 CORRECT PROGRAMS AND
THE LIMITATIONS OF TESTING

Correctness of a program is not an absolute property but a relative property. A program cannot be correct in any absolute sense; it can only be correct relative to some description of what the user would like it to do. This description may exist only in the head of the user or designer, or it may be a completely formal specification. Suppose that f is the function computed by a program p. Then it is possible to imagine the existence of a "correct version" f^* of p that corresponds to the description of what p is supposed to do. To demonstrate that p is correct it is necessary to prove that f is equivalent to f^*. Knowledge of f^* may be informal or restricted to tables of sample values. In testing, it often takes the form of an *oracle* $q(x,p(x))$ which, for each input x to p, is able to determine if $p(x) = f^*(x)$ (i.e., if p gives the correct output for x).

Since programs are run on finite machines over finite input sets, it is possible to prove the correctness of any program by testing it over its whole input domain. In general, domains are so large that they are effectively infinite, so that a practical correctness-proving procedure will not be able to use the finiteness of input domains. For this reason, it will be assumed in the following that all programs are run on machines with arbitrarily large amounts of storage of arbitrary precision.

The most important theoretical result in program testing and analysis is that no general purpose testing and analysis procedure can be used to prove program correctness. This is true regardless of the information available about the correct version f^* of a program function f. It is true even if the complete text of a program p^* implementing f^* were available. This follows directly from the following theorem in which it is proved that it is impossible to construct a general method for determining the equivalence of programs. The equivalence result implies the impossibility of constructing a testing or analysis method for the following reasons. Suppose there were a testing or analysis method that could be used to determine the correctness of an arbitrary program p relative to an arbitrary specification f^*. For any two programs p_1 and p_2, let p_1 be the program and p_2 be the specification. The testing or analysis method could then be used to determine the equivalence of p_1 and p_2. The equivalence theorem will be discussed from several points of view.

Theorem 4.1. There is no program E which, for any two programs p_1 and p_2, has the property that $E(p_1, p_2) = true$ if and only if p_1 is equivalent to p_2.

Proof. Suppose there were such a program E. Then use it to define the following program H which, like E, operates on programs.

```
program H(p₁, p₂)
    if E(E,H) = true then return not(E(p₁, p₂))
                    else return E(p₁, p₂)
endprogram
```

If, for any two programs p_1 and p_2, E and H are equivalent, then H should return the same as E. But when E and H are equivalent they return the opposite result, which is contradictory. So E and H must not be equivalent. But if E and H are not equivalent, H always returns the same value as E which is also contradictory. Hence E must not exist.

Some readers may be uneasy with this proof because it involves the definition of a function in terms of itself. This is possible through the use of sophisticated results in recursion theory. A more familiar approach might be to prove the equivalence of this theorem with the halting problem. Recall that the halting problem states that it is not possible to construct a program T which, for any program p, can determine if p terminates for all input (i.e., does not get caught in an endless loop).

Theorem 4.2. If there exists a program E which can be used to determine the equivalence of any two programs p_1 and p_2, then it is possible to solve the halting problem.

Proof. Suppose that p is any program and use it to define the following program h.

```
program h(x)
    y = p(x)
    return (0)
endprogram
```

Now let z be the zero function (i.e., $z(x)$ terminates and $z(x) = 0$ for all x). Clearly h is equivalent to z if and only if p terminates for all values x since if p does not terminate for some value, then h will not terminate for that value. Hence, if it is possible to determine the equivalence of h and z, it is possible to solve the halting problem for an arbitrary program p.

Finally a direct proof is presented. The direct proof is more complicated, but it gives a deeper understanding of what can and cannot be programmed. In addition, the direct proof is more formal. In the previous proofs, there is no discussion of the ranges and domains of the programs involved. In this proof all programs are programs on the positive integers and their range is restricted to the values true and false. Note that since all such programs are included, some of them will not terminate for some input values (i.e., will get caught in infinite loops).

Direct Proof. Suppose $E(p, q)$ is an equivalence program which takes on the value true if p and q are equivalent and false if they are not. The set of all programs on the integers which give the values true or false can be arranged in a sequence, and can be indexed, so that any such program corresponds to a program p_n in the sequence. For each p_n define another program p'_n such that for all positive integers x, $p'_n(x) = p_n(n)$ (i.e., p'_n is a constant function program). Define the function f to be the program which gives the value false for all positive integers. Now if the equivalence program E exists, it is possible to define the following program g.

> program $g(n)$
>   if $E(p'_n, f) =$ true then return true
>   else return false
>
> endprogram

Now clearly $g(n)$ is a program on the positive integers which gives true or false so that for some index i, $g(n) = p_i(n)$ for all positive integers n. Consider the computation $g(i)$, where g is applied to its index value.

$$g(i) = \text{if } E(p'_i, f) = \text{true then true}$$
$$\text{else false}$$

case (i) $E(p'_i, f) =$ true. This equivalence means that for all positive integers x, $p'_i(x) = f(x) =$ false. Hence, from the definition for p'_i, (i) must be false. But, from the definition of g, if $E(p'_i, f) =$ true, then $g(i) =$ true. Hence, since $g = p_i$, then $p_i(i) =$ true, which is contradictory.

case (ii) $E(p'_i, f) \neq$ true. The lack of equivalence means that for some value x either $p_i'(x)$ does not terminate or terminates with the value true. From the definition for p'_i, this implies that either $p_i(i)$ does not terminate or terminates with the value true. But, from the definition of g, if $E(p'_i, f) \neq$ true, then $g(i) =$ false. Hence, since $g = p_i$, then $p_i(i)$ terminates with the value false, which is contradictory.

Therefore the assumption of the existence of E leads to a contradiction.

4.3 THEORY OF FUNCTIONAL TESTING AND ANALYSIS

The theorems of the previous section prove that there is no mechanical or effective equivalence procedure which can be used to determine if an arbitrary program p computes the function f^* corresponding to an arbitrary program specification. Functional testing and analysis avoids the problem by dividing the validation problem into a set of smaller problems, for which an effective theory can be developed.

Functional testing and analysis is based on assumptions about how a program or system is constructed and on mathematical results from algebra and graph theory. The starting assumption is that programs consist of collections of input-output *functions* which are organized into *structures*, and that program faults are either *functional* or *structural* faults.[1] Functions correspond to expressions, statements, and program paths that are used to compute desired output for given input. Structures correspond to graph-like organizations of functions into interacting sequences. Functional faults correspond to incorrect expressions and result in incorrect input-output behavior. Structural faults correspond to incorrect program or module structures and result in incorrect function sequences or function interactions.

4.3.1 Functional Testing

The importance of functions in programs was emphasized in Chapter 2. Programs can be viewed as consisting of many different functions at varying levels of abstraction and detail. These functions are conceptual units of thought which are used by the programmer during requirements, design, and implementation. Errors in thinking will be associated with errors in these units of thought, and it is therefore necessary to take them into account in any testing or validation method.

It is assumed in functional testing that for each function f implemented by the programmer there is a correct function f^* which is the "correct version" of f. In functional testing a function is executed over selected input, and its output compared with the expected correct output, i.e., the output that would be produced by f^*. This assumes the existence of an *input-output oracle* which, for any input x for f and output $y = f(x)$, can determine if $y = f^*(x)$. The input-output oracle is a source of information about f^* and can take on different forms, including tables, manual calculation, or even another program.

If a function contains a fault, it produces the wrong output for some input. In general, it is difficult to classify incorrect outputs and to construct testing methods for different output classes. What has been more successful is to classify program faults which lead to failures and to construct testing methods that will reveal the presence of such faults. Fault classification in functional testing is based on the ways in which functions are constructed from component subfunctions. Three kinds of functions will be studied: *expressions, conditional functions*, and *iterative functions*.

In expressions, operators are used to combine a set of functions into a new function. The most common example is arithmetic expressions. Suppose, for example, that $f_1(x)$ and $f_2(x)$ are two functions. Then they can be combined in an expression, say

$$(f_1(x)^2 + 2f_2(x))$$

to form a new function.

A Boolean function $b(x)$ and two other functions $f_1(x)$ and $f_2(x)$ can be used to form a conditional function $g(x)$ of the form

$$g(x) = \text{if } b(x) \quad \text{then } f_1(x) \quad \text{else } f_2(x).$$

Iterative functions involve loops. It is also possible to consider recursion, but this will not be covered. Suppose that $b(x)$ and $f(x)$ are two functions of x and $b(x)$ is a Boolean function. Then they can be combined to form the iterative function

$$\text{repeat while } b(x) = \text{true}$$
$$x \leftarrow f(x)$$
$$\text{endrepeat}$$

The "$\leftarrow$" indicates assignment. In this while-loop construct it is assumed the test is done at the beginning of the loop. Iterative synthesis can also be used to form functions using an until-loop construct in which the test is done at the end of the loop.

The rules for test selection which have been developed in functional testing require that each function f implemented in a program be "similar" to the correct function f^*. This will be referred to as the *competent programmer assumption*.[2,3] It is based on the observation that when a programmer sits down to write a program, for example, to sort a file, it is unlikely that he will accidently write a Gaussian elimination routine. More formally, it assumes that for each function f associated with a program, there is a set of functions F_f with the following properties:

(i) f is in F_f.

(ii) f^* is in F_f.

(iii) There is a method for selecting tests for f such that for any f' in F_f, if f and f' agree on these tests, then they are equivalent.

We know from the fundamental results at the beginning of the chapter that the sets F_f cannot be big enough to contain all functions, since it would then be implied that a general purpose equivalence method exists. In practice the sets F_f have to be made very small in order for property (iii) to be fulfilled. They are often defined as being functions which deviate from the given function f in some manner. The allowable deviations depend on what kind of function f is: expression, conditional, or iterative.

In order for testing to be practical, it is necessary for the test method in property (iii) to be *effective* in the sense that there is a mechanical procedure for selecting the tests. In practice this is not always possible and weaker kinds of methods need to be allowed. A test selection method may be *partially effective* if there is a mechanical procedure for determining if a given set of tests has certain properties which are known to be sufficient for proving equivalence of f and f', but there is no known mechanical procedure for constructing the tests in the first place. A test method may also be *statistically effective* if there is a mechanical test generation procedure for constructing tests which have the property that if $f = f'$ over those tests then f and f' are probably equivalent. It is *statistically partially effective* if there is a mechanical method for determining whether a given set of tests has the property that if $f = f'$ over the tests, then they are probably equivalent, but there is no mechanical procedure available for generating those tests. The statistical interpretation of the word "probably" is discussed later in the chapter.

In summary, functional testing is based on the following assumptions:

(i) Functionality principle: programs are collections of expressions, conditional functions, and iterative functions.

(ii) Input-output oracles: there is a way of determining if a program's output for some input is correct.

(iii) Competent programmer assumption: program functions are close enough to correct functions so that there is an effective procedure for determining if they are equivalent.

The theoretical results for functional testing contained later in the chapter consist of mathematical theorems that prove the effectiveness of test selection methods for determining the equivalence of expressions, conditional functions, and iterative functions.

4.3.2   Functional Analysis

In addition to the invention of input-output functions, programmers join functions together into graph-like structures which order the application of interacting functions into sequences. The principal technique of functional analysis is the analysis of these structures, or *structural analysis*. The main difference between an input-output function and a functional structure is in the programmer's understanding or knowledge of how the correct program should operate. In the first case the programmer knows about the output to be expected for selected input, and this information is embedded in an input-output oracle. In the second case the programmer knows about the sequences in which functions should be used during program execution, and this information is modeled by a *function sequence* or *function interface* oracle.

Although the number of possible functional paths through a program structure is potentially infinite, it is possible to define a small finite subset of these so that if a function sequence failure occurs in some path it also occurs in one of the paths in the subset. This makes it possible to base structural analysis on failure analysis rather than fault analysis. It is, in effect, possible to generate tests that will cause any possible sequence failure to occur. For this reason, structural analysis is more powerful than functional testing. Functional testing contains rules for detecting input-output failures that result from a selected class of functional faults. Structural analysis contains rules for detecting any function sequence failure.

In the simplest case, structural analysis analyzes a program to determine sequences of function invocations, and those sequences are verified by a function sequence oracle. Structural analysis rules are used to select the finite subset of paths whose examination is sufficient for the determination of any sequence failure. The oracle can take the form of a directed graph like that in Figure 4.1, in which nodes correspond to functions and arcs to the transfer of control from one function to the next. It specifies that first f_1 must occur, followed by f_2. This must be followed by f_3 or f_4. The function f_3 is always followed by a final application of f_5, and f_4 is followed by a repeated application of f_2.

In practice, structural analysis is more complicated for several reasons. The first is that programs do not generally consist of simple sequences of explicit function calls. They often contain *anonymous* functions corresponding to sections of code which are not encapsulated in a function definition. The programmer's understanding of the sequences in which functions are to be used is likely to be in terms of the sequences of states that are to occur as the result of functional computations rather than in terms of a sequence of explicit function calls. The states may be simple, and consist of the types or flavors of data that occur in variables, or more complex, describing relationships between variables and data structures. Chapter 3 described the kinds of states that can occur in programs and their basic importance in the construction and understanding of programs. Structural analysis examines the sequences of states that occur in the structures used to join functions together into larger components.

The second complication that occurs in structural analysis is due to the nonsingular nature of a programmer's knowledge of the function sequences in a correct program. It is likely that the function sequence oracle will not consist of a single all-embracing structural graph like that in Figure 4.1, but will consist of several graphs, corresponding to different aspects of the program and different levels of functional detail. The approach to structural analysis described later in Chapter 6 is based on a three-level hierarchy of modules, state transformations, and data structure operations. At the top level a program or system is viewed as a collection of interacting modules in which one module "uses" another by calling a function in that module. Structural analysis of module interactions requires a knowledge of the correct-uses structure of the system. At the middle level, a program is viewed

FIGURE 4.1. Function sequences oracle.

as consisting of sequences of type and state transformations. Structural analysis at this level requires a correct-sequence oracle which can be used to determine if state sequences occurring in the program also occur in the correct version of the program. The main problem-solving level of the program is at this middle level, in which one problem-specific state is transformed into another. In order to carry out these transformations the program must store and retrieve data from data structures and files. This is done using data structure operators which are mixed in with the state transformations. Data structures have to be initialized, accessed, and updated in ways that are associated with the correct usage of the structures rather than with the solution to the problem. The third, and bottom, level of function sequence information consists of oracles that describe legal sequences of data structure operations.

Up to this point it has been assumed that structural analysis oracles were available for examining actual sequences of functions or states. In practice all that may be reasonably expected is an interface oracle, from which it is possible to determine if it is legal for one function or state to be immediately followed by another. This turns out to be sufficient for a very general class of problems.

When functions are joined together into structures they interact by passing data to each other. Errors may occur in the details of the data interfaces, resulting in inconsistencies between formal and actual parameters in procedure definitions and uses. Structural analysis includes checking parameter interfaces, as well as function and data sequence interfaces.

The theoretical results that are needed for structural analysis consist of theorems about the sequences of labels occurring on paths through graphs. Some theorems prove that if a specified finite subset of the label sequences in one graph is contained in another graph, then all label sequences in the first graph are contained in the second. Other theorems describe the conditions under which it is sufficient to examine label interfaces. Two node labels interface if they are on nodes connected by a graph arc from one node to the next. Under certain conditions, if all node label interfaces in one graph are also node label interfaces in a second, then all label sequences in the first are label sequences in the second. Similar results can be proved for graphs for which the arcs are labeled, rather than the nodes.

4.3.3 Functional Testing and Analysis Failures

Functional testing and structural analysis are based partly on empirical research and partly on mathematical theory. The empirical research justifies the interpretation of a program as a structural arrangement of expression, and conditional and iterative functions. It also justifies the expectation that oracles will be available and that the competent programmer assumption holds. The theory is used to prove the effectiveness of test selection and path analysis methods. Functional testing and analysis can fail to find an error in the following ways.

(i) Functionality or structural identification failure. This occurs when the analyst fails to identify all the functions and structures used in a program. Attempts to solve this problem with automatic function and structure identification are discussed in Chapters 5 and 6.

(ii) Oracle assumption failure. If no oracle is available for a particular function or structure, testing or analysis cannot be done.

(iii) Fault class failure. This occurs during fault analysis if the program contains a fault that does not fall into any class for which a fault detection method exists. In functional testing it corresponds to a failure in the competent programmer assumption.

The advantages of functional testing and analysis are that it is systematic, allowing a clear explanation of what will or will not be found, and that empirical research indicates that it will detect a large class of faults and errors.[4,5]

4.4 STATISTICAL TESTING

Both functional testing and structural analysis depend on knowledge of the internal structure of a function. Before the discussion of the theoretical results for these methods, *black-box* functions will be considered. For these functions, there is absolutely no knowledge of the internal algebraic or computational structure of the programs which implement them. This is the case during acceptance testing when only the external behavior of the program is to be considered, and none of its design or implementation details. It is assumed that there is an input-output oracle available. The only known systematic testing method in this situation is *statistical testing*.

In statistical testing, tests are selected so that if a program f and its specification f^* agree on the tests, then f and f^* are "probably" equivalent. Note that this does not mean that we can estimate the probability that $f = f^*$, since two functions are either equal or they are not, and the probability of their being equal is a meaningless concept. What we actually estimate is the probability of randomly choosing an input x for which $f(x) = f^*(x)$. There are several possible ways to formally define the concept of probable equivalence. The approach that is discussed here is a variation on hypothesis testing. It is not as formal as other approaches, such as parameter estimation, but it has the advantage that it does not depend on a sophisticated understanding of statistics, and it is practical in the sense that it requires fewer tests than more formal statistical methods.

In all of the testing that is to be discussed as follows, it is assumed that the tests are randomly selected according to the *operational distribution* for the program. This is the probability distribution describing the frequency with which different elements of the input domain are selected when the program is in actual use. Without this assumption the results are not useful. In addition, all testing is done with replacement so that when tests are being selected randomly, it is possible to choose a test that has been previously selected. This is not a problem if the probability of selecting any given input is very small, as is the case for most operational distributions over large sets of input objects. When this is not true the results must be refined by splitting up the input domains.

Suppose that H is an hypothesis which we decide to accept or reject on the basis of the outcome of some experiment. There are two types of errors we can make.

Type 1: reject the hypothesis when it is true

Type 2: accept the hypothesis when it is false

Suppose that the probability of accepting the hypothesis when it is false is small. Then if the outcome of the experiment is such that we accept the hypothesis we can, intuitively, expect that the hypothesis is "probably" true. The following theorem describes the application of hypothesis testing to equivalence of functions.

> **Theorem 4.3.** Suppose that f is a function whose input is selected according to an operational input distribution and let F_f be a set of functions containing f and other functions with the same operational distribution as f. Suppose that f' is some function in F_f and we wish to test for the probable equivalence of f and f'. This can be done as follows. Let θ be the unknown probability that $f \neq f'$ when tested over an input element which is selected according to the operational distribution. Choose h to be such that if $\theta < 1/h$ we can think of f and f' as being probably equivalent. Now consider the following hypothesis H.

$$H: \theta < 1/h$$

Suppose we test f and f' over n tests and do the following. We accept the hypothesis if $f = f'$ over all tests and reject it otherwise. The type 2 error for this hypothesis is more serious than the type 1 error. In the type 2 error we accept that $\theta < 1/h$ when it is not true, that is, we accept that f is probably equal to f' when it is not true. In the type 1 error we reject that $\theta < 1/h$ when in fact it is true. But rejecting the hypothesis only happens if f was found to be unequal to f' on some test, and if this happens we are no longer interested in θ anyway, f is known to be unequal to f'. If

$$n > \log(h)/(\log(h) - \log(h - 1)),$$

then the probability of making a type 2 error is less than $1/h$.

Proof. If we accept the hypothesis and the hypothesis is false, then $\theta \geq 1/h$ and no failures (i.e., $f \neq f'$) were encountered in n tests. The probability of no failures in n tests is

$$(1 - \theta)^n \text{ and since } \theta \geq 1/h$$
$$(1 - \theta)^n \leq (1 - 1/h)^n.$$

Now if $\quad n > \log(h)/(\log(h) - \log(h - 1)),$

then $\quad n(\log(h) - \log(h - 1)) > \log(h)$

$\qquad \log(h/(h - 1))^n > \log(h)$

$\qquad (h/(h - 1))^n > h$

$\qquad ((h - 1)/h)^n < 1/h$

or $\qquad (1 - 1/h)^n < 1/h.$

Hence, the probability of accepting the hypothesis when it is false is less than $1/h$. For sufficiently large h, this can be interpreted to mean that if f and f' agree on $n = \log(h)/(\log(h) - \log(h - 1))$ tests, then f and f' are probably, to within probability $1/h$, equal functions. The result can be made more concise using the inequality [see exercise 4.2].[6]

$$h\log(h) > \log(h)/(\log(h) - \log(h - 1)),$$

so that if f and f' agree on $h\log(h)$ tests then they are probably equal, to within probability $1/h$.

The theorem indicates that a sizable number of tests are needed to do statistical evaluation of equivalence. If we wish to be sure that $f = f'$ to within a probability of 1 in 100, we will need at least 459 tests over which there is no failure.

It is noted that if it is desirable to get an estimate of θ then hypothesis testing can still be used, but the hypothesis acceptance criteria in Theorem 4.3 must be modified. As it stands, the probability of making a type 1 error—saying that the hypothesis is false when it is in fact true—is very high. This is because it results in rejecting $\theta < 1/h$ when only one failure occurs in a sequence of tests. In order to minimize the probability of making a type 1 error, while still keeping the probability of a type 2 error below $1/h$, it is necessary to change the acceptance criteria to: accept H if the number of failures t is less than some value t^*. If an optimal value of t^* is found, one that minimizes the probability of a type 1 error while still keeping the probability of a type 2 error below $1/h$, then t/n, where n is the number of tests, becomes a reasonable estimate of θ, the failure rate.

4.5 EXPRESSION FUNCTIONS

The detection of faults in functions formed using expressions depends on the existence of tests that can determine if two algebraic expressions are equivalent. Algebra can be used to define broad classes of functions F for which there are effective equivalence procedures. The first results that are included here are very simple, and for very simple classes F. This is followed by some more powerful methods, but ones that require large numbers of tests. Finally, some statistically effective methods are given which only require testing over a single test point. The first theorem is used to detect faults where an expression is "off by a constant."

In the following discussion a *polynomial* is a function of a single variable. A polynomial form in several variables is referred to as a *multinomial*.

Theorem 4.4. Suppose that f is a rational form:

$$\frac{f_1(x_1,x_2,\ldots x_n)}{f_2(x_1, x_2,\ldots x_n)}$$

where f_1 and f_2 are multinomials in x_i, $1 \leq i \leq n$. Let F_f contain f and any other rational form which differs from f in exactly one of its constant coefficients. A test is nonzero if all variable values are nonzero (i.e., $x_i \neq 0$, $1 \leq i \leq n$). The equivalence of f' and f can be determined with a single nonzero test for which f and f' are both defined and do not evaluate to zero.

Proof. Suppose f' is the rational form

$$\frac{f'_1(x_1,x_2,\ldots,x_n)}{f'_2(x_1,x_2,\ldots,x_n)}$$

and that f and f' are defined and nonzero for some nonzero test. If $f = f'$ on the test, then, since f and f' differ by at most a single coefficient in either (but not both) their denominators or numerators, $f'_1 = f_1$ and $f'_2 = f_2$ on the test. Assume that f_1 and f'_1 are the same except for some coefficient. Then all of their terms in $x_1,x_2,\ldots,x_n$ are the same except for one. These must be equal at the test point but the fact that the test point is nonzero implies their coefficients are also the same. A similar argument holds for the case where f_2 and f'_2 are the same except for some coefficient. Hence f and f' are identical rational forms.

In the case where f and f' are simple polynomials in a single variable, much broader classes of functions F can be defined using the following well-known result from algebra.

Theorem 4.5. Suppose that F contains all polynomials of degree less than or equal to k and suppose that f and f' are in F. Then if f and f' agree on any set of $k + 1$ different values, they are identical polynomials.

Definition. Suppose f is a multinomial in the variables x_i, $1 \leq i \leq k$. Then f can be written as a sum of terms t_i:

$$f = \sum_{i=1}^{s} a_i t_i$$

where each t_i is a unique product of powers of $x_1, x_2,\ldots,x_k$ and each a_i is a constant. If $t - 1$ is the largest exponent in f, then f will have at most $s = t^k$ terms. Each term t_i is a function $t_i(x_1,x_2,\ldots,x_k)$ over the same domain as f. Let $(c_1,c_2,\ldots,c_k)$ be some element of the domain and let V be the vector

$$V = (t_1(c_1,c_2,\ldots,c_k),t_2(c_{1,2},\ldots,c_k),\ldots,t_s(c_1,c_2,\ldots,c_k)).$$

The elements of V are the *components* of f at $(c_1,c_2,\ldots,c_k)$.

Theorem 4.6. Suppose that f and f' are two multinomials in x_i, $1 \le i \le k$, and assume that they both have the same s terms. Let $(c_{i,1},c_{i,2},\ldots,c_{i,k})$, $1 \le i \le s$, be s elements in the domain of f and f', and let the elements of the vectors V_i, $1 \le i \le s$, be the components of f at $(c_{i,1}, c_{i,2},\ldots,c_{i,k})$. Let T be the s by s matrix whose rows are the vectors V_i. Suppose that the elements $(c_{i,1}, c_{i,2},\ldots,c_{i,k})$ have the following properties.

(i) $f = f'$ over the elements $(c_{i,1}, c_{i,2},\ldots,c_{i,k})$, $1 \le i \le s$, and
(ii) the matrix T is nonsingular.

Then f and f' are equivalent.

Proof. Suppose

$$f = \sum_{i=1}^{s} a_i t_i \text{ and } f' = \sum_{i=1}^{s} b_i t_i$$

and let A and B be the column vectors

$$A = \begin{bmatrix} a_1 \\ a_2 \\ . \\ . \\ a_s \end{bmatrix} \quad \text{and} \quad B = \begin{bmatrix} b_1 \\ b_2 \\ . \\ . \\ b_s \end{bmatrix}$$

$$f = f' \text{ over } (c_{i,1},c_{i,2},\ldots,c_{i,k}), \ 1 \le i \le s,$$

implies that

$$TA = TB,$$

and T nonsingular implies $A = B$.

The following corollary restates the theorem for the simple case where the multinomials are linear.

Corollary. Suppose that f and f' are linear multinomials in the variables $x_1, x_2, \ldots, x_{s-1}$, that is, they are of the form $a_1 x_1 + a_2 x_2 + \ldots + a_{s-1} x_{s-1} + a_s$. Let T be the s by s matrix in Figure 4.2.
    Suppose that $f = f'$ over each test T_i, $1 \le i \le s$,
where

$$T_i = (x_{i,1},x_{i,2},\ldots,x_{i,s-1}).$$

Then if T is nonsingular f and f' are identical multinomials.

$$T = \begin{bmatrix} x_{1,1} & x_{1,2} & \cdots & x_{1,s-1} & 1 \\ x_{2,1} & x_{2,2} & \cdots & x_{2,s-1} & 1 \\ & & \cdot & & \\ & & \cdot & & \\ & & \cdot & & \\ x_{s,1} & x_{s,2} & \cdots & x_{s,s-1} & 1 \end{bmatrix}$$

FIGURE 4.2. Linear multinomials test matrix.

The corollary indicates that it is possible to prove the equivalence of two linear multinomials in $s - 1$ variables with only s tests. The previous theorem indicated that the equivalence of two arbitrary nonlinear multinomials f and f' in $s - 1$ variables can be proved in s tests where s is the number of elementary terms in which f and f' can be written.

These results can be used to define sets of functions F for which there is a partially effective equivalence method. The same sets also have an effective equivalence method, but at the cost of much larger test sets. Suppose that f_1 and f_2 are two multinomial functions in the variables $x_1, x_2, \ldots, x_k$ and that $t - 1$ is the largest exponent in either f_1 or f_2. Then the equivalence of f_1 and f_2 can be determined by testing them over a set of k-tuples forming a *cascade* set of degree t.

Definition. Let C be a set of k-tuples and suppose that $(x_1, x_2, \ldots, x_i, \ldots, x_k)$ is a k-tuple in C. Then the *successors* of the i-tuple $(x_1, x_2, \ldots, x_i)$ consist of the set of all elements x_{i+1} such that for some $(x'_{i+2}, \ldots, x'_k)$ the k-tuple $(x_1, x_2, \ldots, x_i, x_{i+1}, x'_{i+2}, \ldots, x'_k)$ is in C. C is a *cascade set of degree t* if:

(i) there are t elements x_1 which occur as the first element of some k-tuple $(x_1, x_2, \ldots, x_k)$ and

(ii) for each k-tuple $(x_1, x_2, \ldots, x_i, \ldots, x_k)$ and each i, $1 \le i \le k$, the successors of $(x_1, x_2, \ldots, x_i)$ are a set of t elements.

Theorem 4.7. Suppose that f_1 and f_2 are two multinomials in k variables. Let $t - 1$ be the largest exponent in f_1 and f_2. If $f_1 = f_2$ over a cascade set C of k-tuples of degree t, then f_1 and f_2 are identical multinomials.

Proof. This can be proved using the result for polynomials in a single variable. The proof is by induction on k. For $k = 1$ it is the familiar single variable polynomial result. Suppose it is true for multinomials of degree $k - 1$ and let f_1 and f_2 be two multinomials of degree k. Now f_1 and f_2 can be written as polynomials in x_k in which the coefficient of each power of x_k is a multinomial in $x_1, x_2, \ldots, x_{k-1}$. If C is a cascade set of degree t of k-tuples then it can be constructed from a cascade set C' of degree t of $(k - 1)$-tuples in the following way. For each $(k - 1)$-tuple in C', construct t k-tuples by adding t values for x_k. For each $(k - 1)$-tuple in C', the coefficients of f_1 and f_2, written as polynomials in x_k, will evaluate to a constant. So for each such $(k - 1)$-tuple, $f_1 = f_2$ over the t associated values for x_k used to construct the corresponding

k-tuples in C. This implies that f_1 is identical to f_2 over those t values which implies they have identical coefficients. Hence the coefficients of f_1 and f_2 evaluate to the same constants for all $(k - 1)$-tuples in C'. Since C' is a cascade set of $(k - 1)$-tuples of degree t, the inductive hypothesis implies that the multinomials which are the coefficients of f_1 and f_2 when written as polynomials in x_k must be equivalent, and hence f_1 and f_2 are equivalent.

The problem with cascade sets is that they grow very quickly. Suppose, for example, that a set F corresponds to multinomials of degree at most 2 in 4 variables. The cascade set required for equivalence will have 3^4 $= 81$ tests. In general a cascade set of k-tuples of degree t has t^k elements. The multinomial results previously described can be extended to more complex algebraic forms, including those containing fractional exponents, but the sizes of the required cascade sets are enormous.[7] This suggests that in general, more restrictive assumptions will be needed for the sets F, and hence for the class of program faults that can be detected. An alternative is the use of a statistically effective method.

Statistically effective equivalence of algebraic forms is based on the following observation. Suppose that f_1 and f_2 are two polynomials of degree at most n and that $f_1 = f_2$ over a randomly chosen value x. Now $f_1 = f_2$ means that $f_1 - f_2 = 0$ at x, and hence that x is a root of $f_1 - f_2$, a polynomial of degree at most n. Such a polynomial has at most n roots unless it is identically zero. The probability of choosing one of n points in a random selection from an effectively infinite set of points is arbitrarily small, and hence if $f_1 = f_2$ at a randomly chosen point, f_1 and f_2 are almost certainly the same polynomial. This was observed by DeMillo.[8] This result can be extended to multinomials in several variables.

Theorem 4.8. Suppose that f_1 and f_2 are two multinomials in the variables x_1, $x_2,\ldots,x_n$. Then a statistically effective equivalence procedure is to compare f_1 and f_2 on randomly chosen input data.

Proof: The proof will be informal. Consider the multinomial $g = f_1 - f_2$. Now g is a multinomial in $(x_1,x_2,\ldots,x_n)$. Choose a random point and evaluate g. If g does not evaluate to zero, then $f_1 \neq f_2$. Suppose g evaluates to zero. If g is not identically zero (i.e., zero on all data), then the subspace of n-dimensional space over which g is zero is an $(n - k)$-dimensional space where $k \geq 1$. For example, if $n = 1$, the subspace is a finite set of points on the x_1 axis. If $n = 2$, the subspace is a curve in the (x_1, x_2) plane. The size, or *measure*, of an $(n - k)$-dimensional space embedded in an n-dimensional space is effectively zero so that the probability of having randomly chosen a point $(x_1, x_2, \ldots,x_n)$ at which g evaluates to zero, and hence $f_1 = f_2$, is arbitrarily small, unless g is identically zero. Therefore $f_1 = f_2$ can be concluded with high confidence if $f_1 = f_2$ at a randomly chosen data point.

The result can also be extended to rational forms (multinomial fractions) and multinomials with fractional exponents.

Theorem 4.9. Suppose $f = f_1/f_2$ and $g = g_1/g_2$ are two rational forms where f_1, f_2, g_1, and g_2 are multinomials in the variables $x_1, x_2, \ldots, x_n$. Then it is a statistically partially effective equivalence procedure to compare f and g at randomly chosen input data for which both f and g are defined (i.e., f_2 and g_2 do not evaluate to zero).

Proof. Suppose that f_1/f_2 and g_1/g_2 are not equivalent for those data points for which they are both defined. Consider the probability of choosing at random a point on which they are both defined and are equal. This is the probability of choosing a point on which $f_1g_2 - f_2g_1$ is zero and at which f_2 and g_2 are not zero. Now if there are points at which f_1/f_2 and g_1/g_2 are both defined and are not equal, there are points at which $f_1g_2 - f_2g_1$ is not zero and f_2 and g_2 are not zero. Hence $f_1g_2 - f_2g_1$ is not identically zero. The probability of choosing at random a point at which $f_1g_2 - f_2 g_1$ is zero is therefore negligible and hence the probability of choosing a point at which not only $f_1g_2 - f_2g_1$ is zero but also f_2 and g_2 are not zero is also negligible.

A *radical* is a multinomial with noninteger, rational exponents. A radical form is a rational form (i.e., algebraic fraction) involving radicals. The following is an example of a radical form

$$\frac{x^{1/2} + y^{1/2}}{y^2 - xy^{1/2}}$$

Theorem 4.10. Suppose f and g are two radical forms in the variables x_1, $x_2, \ldots, x_n$. Then it is a statistically partially effective equivalence procedure to compare f and g on randomly chosen input data for which both f and g are defined.

Proof. The partial aspect of the effectiveness may be more relevant here than in the previous theorem because if the range of the functions does not include imaginary numbers, the forms may become undefined for reasons other than the denominator of a fraction evaluating to zero (e.g., square root of a negative number). However, since only partial effectiveness is claimed, this is not discussed.

The proof method is that of rationalizing factors. Suppose that

$$f = \frac{f_1}{f_2} \qquad \text{and} \qquad g = \frac{g_1}{g_2}$$

where f_1, f_2, g_1, and g_2 are radicals. Let

$$h = \frac{h_1}{h_2} = f - g = \frac{f_1g_2 - g_1f_2}{f_2g_2}$$

It is possible to construct nonzero radical multinomials h_1' and h_2' so that $h_1 * h_1'$ and $h_2 * h_2'$ are nonradical, nonzero multinomials. A proof of this can be found in the references.[7] The following example illustrates the basic idea of rationalizing factors for the above example of a radical form.

$$\frac{x^{1/2} + y^{1/2}}{y^2 - xy^{1/2}} * \frac{x^{1/2} - y^{1/2}}{y^2 + xy^{1/2}} = \frac{x - y}{y^4 - x^2 y}$$

Suppose that f and g are not equivalent for that data for which they are defined. Consider the probability of choosing at random a point at which they are both defined and equal. This is the probability of choosing a point at which $h = f - g$ is zero and $h_2 = f_2 g_2$ is not zero. If f and g are not equivalent then h is not identically zero. Using the method of rationalizing factors construct nonzero radicals h_1' and h_2' so that

$$h * h' = \frac{h_1}{h_2} * \frac{h_1'}{h_2'}$$

is a rational form involving nonradical multinomials. If h is zero then $h * h'$ is zero. Since h is not identically zero, and h_1' and h_2' are not identically zero, then $h * h'$ is a nonradical, nonzero rational form. Hence the probability of choosing a point at random at which $f = g$ and f_2 and g_2 do not evaluate to zero is the probability of choosing at random a point at which $h * h'$ evaluates to zero and h_2 does not evaluate to zero, or $h * h'$ is not defined. If $h * h'$ is not defined then $h_2 * h_2'$, a nonzero multinomial, evaluates to zero. So we have the probability that either one nonzero multinomial, $h * h'$, evaluates to zero, or the probability that another nonzero multinomial, $h_2 * h_2'$, evaluates to zero. Both of these are, by Theorem 4.9, negligible probabilities. Hence, to suppose that f is not equivalent to g, when they are defined and equal on a randomly chosen point, implies the occurrence of an event with negligible probability.

4.6 NONARITHMETIC EXPRESSIONS

All of the theorems in the previous sections are for arithmetic expressions. It is possible to consider other kinds of expressions as well. This is not a well-explored area, but it is likely that results can be developed for string, list, and other sorts of operations. Results for Lisp functions can be found in Brooks[9] and for decision table functions in Budd et al.[10] The following theorems describe some obvious results for data storage and retrieval operations.

Let $C = \{c_1, c_2, \ldots, c_n\}$ be a set of *storage cells* and let s_i, $1 \le i \le n$, and r_i, $1 \le i \le n$, be *storage* and *retrieval* functions. Assume that the cells of C have values stored in them and that C can be referenced as a data structure. For each i, $s_i(k, C)$ stores the object k in cell c_i of structure C and returns the new value of C. For each i, $r_i(C)$ returns as a value the object stored in cell i of structure C. Let *contents*(c_i) denote the value stored in c_i.

Theorem 4.11. Let F be the set of storage functions for storage structures C of size n, each of whose cells contains some value. Then an effective equivalence procedure for comparing any given storage function s_k with any storage function f in F_f is to test s_k and f with a structure C and a value x such that

$$x \ne contents\ (c_k).$$

Theorem 4.12. Let F be the set of retrieval functions for a storage structure C of size n, each of whose cells contains a value. Then an effective equivalence procedure for F is to test any pair of functions f_1 and f_2 in F with a structure C such that

$$\text{for } i \neq j, \quad contents(c_i) \neq contents(c_j), 1 \leq i < j \leq n.$$

Suppose that f is a function which operates on storage structures C such that each application of f to a structure C results in a sequence of operations on C of the following form:

$$s_i(r_k(C),C), 1 \leq i \leq n, 1 \leq k \leq n.$$

Then f is a *data shuffle function*.

Theorem 4.13. Let F be the set of data shuffle functions for a storage structure C of size n. Then an effective equivalence procedure for F is to test any pair of functions f_1 and f_2 in F with a structure C such that all the stored data objects are different, that is,

$$i \neq j \text{ implies} \quad contents(c_i) \neq contents(c_j), 1 \leq i < j \leq n.$$

4.7 CONDITIONAL AND ITERATIVE FUNCTIONS

This section contains the basic results used to test functions formed by either conditional or iterative synthesis. Suppose that f is a conditional function formed from the Boolean function b and the then and else functions f_1 and f_2. If there is an error in f then the wrong function f_1 or f_2 is selected by b. So it will be assumed that the faults that can occur in the function f are the same as those that can occur in b.

Theorem 4.14. Suppose that f is the function:

$$\text{if } b \text{ then } f_1 \text{ else } f_2.$$

Suppose that B_b is a class of Boolean functions containing b, and T is a test set which can be used to distinguish b from any nonequivalent function b' in B_b. For convenience, assume that b, f_1, and f_2 are all functions of the same variables. Let F_f contain f and all functions which can be constructed from f by substituting some b' from B_b for b in f. Suppose that, for all x in T, $f_1(x) \neq f_2(x)$. Then T can be used to distinguish any two nonequivalent functions f and f' in F_f.

Proof. Suppose $f(x) = f'(x)$ for all x in T. Let b and b' be the Boolean decision functions in f and f'. If $b \neq b'$, then $b(x) \neq b'(x)$ for some test x in T. But $f_1(x) \neq f_2(x)$ implies f and f' will give different output for x, since both f and f' have the same then and else functions f_1 and f_2.

A similar result can be proved for iterative while or until functions, except the required conditions on the test set are more complex. First the general case will be considered, and then a simplified case that is possible for while loops.

Suppose that f is a function of the form:

$$\text{repeat while } b(x) = \text{true}$$
$$x \leftarrow g(x)$$
$$\text{endrepeat}$$

or of the form:

$$\text{repeat until } b(x) = \text{false}$$
$$x \leftarrow g(x)$$
$$\text{endrepeat.}$$

Recall that in a while loop the test is made at the beginning of the loop and in an until loop it is made at the end. Errors in f correspond to iterating the loop the wrong number of times. As in conditional functions, faults that can occur in f are those that can occur in the Boolean b.

Theorem 4.15. Suppose that f is a while or until iterative function constructed from g and b, and that B_b is a set of Boolean functions containing b and defined over the same domain as b. Suppose that there is a set of tests T which has the following properties:

(i) For all b' in B_b not equal to b there is some $x \in T$ and some n such that

$$b(g^i(x)) = \text{true for } i < n$$
$$b(g^n(x)) \neq b'(g^n(x)).$$

If f is a while loop, $n \geq 0$, and if an until loop, $n \geq 1$.
(ii) For $i \neq j$, and all x in T,

$$g^i(x) \neq g^j(x).$$

Let F_f be the set of iterative functions (while if f is while and until if f is until) which can be constructed from g and any Boolean function b' in B. Then T can be used to distinguish any f' in F_f, which is not equivalent to f, from f.

Proof. Suppose f' is in F_f and $f' \neq f$ so that b', the Boolean in f', is not equivalent to b. Then there is an $x \in T$ such that

$$b(g^i(x)) = \text{true for } i < n.$$

This means that the loop in f does not terminate for x before the nth iteration. If f' terminates before the nth iteration, then property (ii) of the theorem implies that f and f' return different values. Assume f' does not terminate before the nth iteration. Then

$$b(g^n(x)) \neq b'(g^n(x))$$

implies that either f or f' terminates but not both and, again, property (ii) implies that $f(x) \neq f'(x)$.

The requirements on T in Theorem 4.15 are much more complicated than in Theorem 4.14 but, upon close analysis, not that unreasonable. Requirement (ii), that

$$g^i(x) \neq g^j(x) \text{ for } i \neq j \text{ and all } x \in T,$$

means only that after each iteration of the loop, x contains a new value. This, or variations that still allow the theorem, is not unreasonable. Requirement (i) means we have to find some y values that will distinguish b from any nonequivalent b' in B_b and then find some x's so that $g^n(x)$ gives these y's and $b(g^i(x))$ is true for i less than n. This may be complicated to figure out. In the case of while loops, there is a simple version of this, based on the fact that the test in the while loop is done before the loop is entered.

> **Corollary.** Suppose that f is a while iterative function constructed from g and b and that B_b is a set of Boolean functions which contains b and which is defined over the same domain as b. Suppose that there is a set of tests T with the following properties:
>
> **(i)** For all b' in B_b there is some $x \in T$ such that
>
> $$b(x) \neq b'(x).$$
>
> **(ii)** For all x in T
>
> $$g^i(x) \neq g^j(x), i \neq j, i \geq 0, j \geq 0.$$
>
> Let F_f be the set of iterative while functions formed from g and any Boolean b' in B. Then for any f' in F_f not equivalent to f there is a test x in T such that $f(x) \neq f'(x)$.

Theorems 4.14 and 4.15 indicate that testing of conditional and iterative functions depends on rules for testing Boolean functions. The following sections are devoted to Boolean functions computed by ordering relations of the form

$$operand \qquad relation \qquad operand$$

where *relation* is $=$, $\neq$, $<$, $\leq$, $>$, or $\geq$. The first set of results involves order relations of the form

$$exp \qquad relation \qquad 0$$

where *exp* is an algebraic expression.
Examples of arithmetic relations include

$$x^2 - y^2 < 0$$
$$w = 0 \qquad \text{and}$$
$$x + 2y = 0.$$

Programs can contain Boolean functions constructed from systems of relations as well as single relations. Equivalence theorems for systems of relations is a topic of current research and only very simple examples will be presented. Fortunately, most systems of relations which define a Boolean function in a program are very simple, and simple techniques are sufficient.

4.7.1 Partially Effective Equivalence Rules for General Classes of Relations

The first set of theorems establishes partially effective equivalence results for arbitrarily complex arithmetic relations but very restricted classes of functions F.

The first result depends on the concept of the smallest number larger than zero that can be taken on by an expression. If the expression is an integer, this will be at least 1, but it could be larger. If the expression is real valued, then let this be denoted by ϵ, where ϵ is the smallest nonzero quantity that will be distinguished from zero. It could be, for example, the smallest number representable on the machine in use. In practice, ϵ can stand for the smallest required degree of discrimination between numbers. Two numbers that differ by less than ϵ will be considered to be effectively equal.

For an arbitrary expression the terms in Figure 4.3 will be used to denote the above constants.

Theorem 4.16. Suppose that f is the arithmetic relation

$$exp \quad rel \quad 0$$

and let F_f consist of all relations of the form

$$exp + k \quad rel \quad 0$$

where k is an integer constant. Then the equivalence of f with any other arithmetic relation $f\,'$ in F_f can be tested using tests that cause the expression in the relation to take on the values in the table in Figure 4.4. Note that different values are needed for different relational operators.

Proof. The proof will be given for the relational operator $<$. The proofs for the other operators are similar.

If $exp + k < 0$ when $exp = maxneg$, then the two functions f and $f\,'$ will give equivalent results for all data for which exp evaluates to a negative number. Otherwise, if $exp + k \geq 0$, the two functions are not equivalent, and

maxneg	=	the maximum value of the expression which is less than zero
maxnonpos	=	the maximum value of the expression which is less than or equal to zero
minpos	=	the minimum value of the expression which is greater than zero
minnonneg	=	the minimum value of the expression which is greater than or equal to zero

FIGURE 4.3. Expression testing constants.

operator	expression values
<	*maxneg, minnonneg*
≤	*maxnonpos, minpos*
>	*maxnonpos, minpos*
≥	*maxneg, minnonneg*
=	zero
≠	zero

FIGURE 4.4. Equivalence proving test values.

the data for which *exp* evaluates to *maxneg* distinguishes between them. If *exp* + k ≥ 0 when *exp* = *minnonneg*, then f and f' are equivalent for data for which *exp* evaluates to a nonnegative value. Otherwise the two functions are not equivalent, and the data for which *exp* evaluates to *minnonneg* reveals this. Hence, the testing of f over *maxneg* and *minnonneg* will determine if f and f' are equivalent.

The results of the previous theorem can be condensed, and the dependence on the choice of test data on the relational operator eliminated as follows.

Corollary. Let f and F_f be as in Theorem 4.16. The equivalence of f with any other arithmetic relation f' in F_f can be tested using tests that cause the expression *exp* in f to take on the values

maxneg, zero, and *minpos*.

The next result is associated with wrong-relation operators in the same way that Theorem 4.16 is associated with off-by-a-constant errors.

Theorem 4.17. Suppose that f is the arithmetic relation

$$exp \quad rel \quad 0$$

where *rel* is one of the relations <, ≤, >, ≥, =, or ≠ and *exp* is an arithmetic expression. Let F_f be the set of all such relations which have the same expression *exp* as f but possibly having a different relational operator *rel*. Then the equivalence of f with any other relation f' in F_f can be tested using tests that cause *exp* to take values such that *exp* < 0, *exp* = 0, and *exp* > 0.

Proof. Consider the table in Figure 4.5. For each possible relational operator *rel* it shows what the outcome of *exp* *rel* 0 would be for data for which *exp* < 0, *exp* = 0, and *exp* > 0. For every possible pair of operators *rel* and *rel'*, there is at least one test where f' will differ from f.

It is possible that either because of the properties of the expression *exp*, or because of a restricted domain of values over which expressions are to be evaluated, that it is not possible to choose data for which *exp* will be either positive, zero, or negative. It turns out to be sufficient to cause *exp* to evaluate to as many of these cases as possible, and the resulting modified version of

	$<$	$\leq$	$>$	$\geq$	$=$	$\neq$
$exp < 0$	true	true	false	false	false	true
$exp = 0$	false	true	false	true	true	false
$exp > 0$	false	false	true	true	false	true

FIGURE 4.5.   Relational function outcomes for different tests.

the theorem is still true. Consider the case where it is possible to cause $exp = 0$ and $exp > 0$, but not $exp < 0$. If there is no data which will cause exp to be negative, then examination of the table in Figure 4.5 indicates that it is not possible to distinguish between the relations using $>$ and $\neq$ and between those using $\leq$ and $=$. Now if there is no data which will cause exp to be negative, then the two relational functions $exp > 0$ and $exp \neq 0$ are logically equivalent over all possible input data. Similarly $exp \leq 0$ is logically equivalent to $exp = 0$. Hence it is not necessary for an equivalence procedure to find data to distinguish between them since, if there is no data for which exp is negative, they are equivalent.

Theorem 4.17 and the corollary of Theorem 4.16 can be combined in the following theorem.

Theorem 4.18.   Suppose that f is an arithmetic relation of the form

$$exp \quad rel \quad 0$$

where rel is $<$, $\leq$, $>$, $\geq$, $=$, or $\neq$ and exp is an arithmetic expression. Let F_f be the set of all relational functions of this form with the same arithmetic expression exp as f but with one of the other possible relational operators, or with the same relational operator as f but with an arithmetic expression $exp + k$ which differs from that in f by an additive constant k. Then the equivalence of f with any relation f' in F_f can be tested for using a set of tests that causes exp to take on the values $maxneg$, zero, and $minpos$, where $maxneg$ and $minpos$ are as defined in Figure 4.3. In the case where exp is real valued, the values correspond to $-\epsilon$, 0, and ϵ.

These results are derived from work described in the list of references.[11,12] The next result can be used to distinguish between relational expressions that differ only in their variables.

Theorem 4.19.   Suppose that f is the arithmetic relation

$$exp \quad rel \quad 0$$

where exp is an arithmetic expression. Let f be the Boolean function computed by the relation. Let w_j, $1 \leq j \leq m$, be m variables not in exp. Define F_f to be the set containing f and all functions f' which can be derived from the relation for f by substituting a w_j for all instances of some variable in exp. Then the equivalence of f with any other function f' in F_f can be tested using a set of three tests which have the following properties:

(i) *exp rel* 0 is true on at least one test and false on at least one test, and either

(ii) *exp'*, the *exp* part of *f '*, is negative on all three tests or positive on all three tests, or

(iii) if exp_1, exp_2, and exp_3 are the values of *exp* on the three tests and exp'_1, exp'_2, and exp'_3 the values of *exp'*, then (exp'_1, exp'_2, exp'_3) is a permutation of (exp_1, exp_2, exp_3) in which every element of (exp_1, exp_2, exp_3) has been moved. There are two such permutations:

$(exp'_1, exp'_2, exp'_3) = (exp_2, exp_3, exp_1)$ (left shift) and
$(exp'_1, exp'_2, exp'_3) = (exp_3, exp_1, exp_2)$ (right shift).

Proof. If *exp'* < 0 on all three tests, then it will differ from *exp* on at least one, since on at least one test *exp rel* 0 is true and on at least one test *exp rel* 0 is false. But on all three tests *exp'* < 0 implies *exp rel* 0 is either true or false on all three tests. A similar argument can be given for *exp'* > 0 on all three tests.

Suppose $(exp'_1, exp'_2, exp'_3) = (exp_2, exp_3, exp_1)$. Let (f'_1, f'_2, f'_3) and (f_1, f_2, f_3) be the outcome of the two associated relations on these tests. Now if *f '* is not different from *f* on at least one test, then

$$(f'_1, f'_2, f'_3) = (f_2, f_3, f_1) = (f_1, f_2, f_3)$$

which implies that $f_1 = f_2 = f_3$ which contradicts the requirements that *f* be true on at least one test and false on at least one test.

Combining Theorem 4.19 with the previous theorems produces the following theorem.

Theorem 4.20. Suppose that *f* is the arithmetic relation

$$exp \quad rel \quad 0$$

where *rel* is an arithmetic operator and *exp* an arithmetic expression. Let $w_j, 1 \le j \le m$, be variables which do not appear in *exp*. Let F_f contain *f*, the function computed by the given relation and all functions *f '* which can be derived from *f* by one of the following:

(i) replacement of *rel* with some other operator *rel'*,

(ii) addition of a constant to *exp*, or

(iii) replacement of all instances of a variable in *exp* by some w_j, $1 \le j \le m$.

Then the equivalence of *f* with any *f '* in F_f can be tested with three tests which cause *exp* to take on the values *maxneg*, zero, and *minpos*, and which cause *exp'* to satisfy either of the following:

(i) *exp'* is either positive on all three tests or negative on all three tests, or

(ii) if (exp_1, exp_2, exp_3) are the values of *exp* on the tests and (exp'_1, exp'_2, exp'_3) are the values of *exp'* on the tests, then (exp'_1, exp'_2, exp'_3) is either the left- or right-shift permutation of (exp_1, exp_2, exp_3).

4.7.2 Effective Equivalence Rules
for Discrete Relations

The previous theorems can be applied to arbitrary arithmetic relations. The following theorems are for relations over ordered discrete domains. They have the advantage of being effective rather than partially effective.

A discrete ordered domain is an ordered sequence such as the positive integers, alphabetic letters, or the truth values $\{0,1\}$, corresponding to false and true. For simplicity assume that all ordered sets are contiguous sequences of nonnegative integers, such as $\{0,1\}$ or $\{1,2,3,4,5\}$. This assumption allows the use of the arithmetic relational results of the previous section. It is assumed in the following theorems that all variables are defined over the same ordered domain.

The theorems in this and in the following section are for very simple relations of the form

$$x \; rel \; y \quad or \quad x \; rel \; k$$

where x and y are variables and k is a constant in the ordered domain. This is not a prohibitive restriction since most discrete domain predicates are this simple, even when the variable domain in the program is the integers. The suggested test values in the following theorem were derived in Foster.[13] The proof uses the theorems given when possible, but requires additional discussion for several special cases (e.g., test value domain is finite and a selected test value is maximal or minimal).

Theorem 4.21. Let f be a relation of the form:

$$x \; rel \; y \quad or \quad x \; rel \; k,$$

where rel is the relational operator $<$, $\leq$, $>$, $\geq$, $=$, or $\neq$, x and y take on values in a discrete sequence, and k is a constant in the sequence. Let w_j, $1 \leq j \leq m$, be any other variables taking on these values and let F_f be the set of functions containing f and all other functions defined by relations in which either rel in f is replaced by some other operator, or x or y are replaced by some w_j. Let f' be an arbitrary member of F_f. Then the following procedure can be used to determine the equivalence of f and f'.

(a) $x \; rel \; y$. If the sequence has three or more elements, choose tests $(x,y,w_j) = (d-1,d,e)$, (d,d,e), $(d,d-1,e)$ where $e < d-1$ or $e > d$. Note that e is intended to be assigned to all w_j, $1 \leq j \leq m$, so that regardless of which w_j was substituted for x or y to form f', only three tests are needed.

If the discrete ordered sequence has only two values, the choice of tests will depend on the relation rel in f. Assume the two values are d and $d+1$. Then for the relation $\leq$ or $>$, choose the tests

$$(x,y,w_j) = (d,d,d+1), (d,d+1,d), (d+1,d,d+1).$$

For the other relations, choose the tests

$$(x,y,w_j) = (d,d,d+1), (d,d+1,d+1), (d+1,d,d).$$

(b) x *rel* k. If the discrete value sequence has three or more elements, and k is nonmaximal, choose

$$(x,w_j) = (k - 1,k), (k,k + 1), (k + 1,k - 1).$$

If k is maximal, choose the tests

$$(x,w_j) = (k - 1,k), (k,k - 1)$$

and if k is minimal,

$$(x,w_j) = (k,k + 1), (k + 1,k).$$

Note that those tests suffice for the special case where $k = 0$ or 1 and the discrete value sequence is $\{0,1\}$.

Proof. (a) x *rel* y. If the sequence has three or more elements, the suggested tests will have the properties required for the application of Theorem 4.18. This is because $x - y$, which becomes *exp* in the theorem, will take on the values $(-1,0,1) = (maxneg,zero,minpos)$, and exp', the result of substituting w_j for x or y, will be either less than zero on all three tests, or greater than zero on all three tests.

Suppose that the sequence has only two elements. Consider the table in Figure 4.6. The first column shows the outcomes for the three suggested tests of x *rel* y. The second and third show the outcomes for w_j *rel* y and x *rel* w_j. The table is divided horizontally into two parts since, depending on the relation *rel* in f, different tests must be used. To simplify the table, it is assumed that the two possible values d and $d + 1$ are 0 and 1. The letters f and t in the table stand for false and true. Every possible pair of entries in the first column differs in at least one test outcome so relations differing in their relational operator will have a different outcome on at least one test. Column one of each row contains a different test output for at least one test from the corresponding outcome in columns two or three of the row so that relations differing in a variable will differ on at least one test.

(b) x *rel* k. Suppose k is nonmaximal, and the sequence has three or more elements. Then the suggested tests will have the properties required by Theorem 4.20. This is because $x - k$ will take on the values $(-1,0,1) = (maxneg,zero,minpos)$ and (exp_1', exp_2', exp_3'), the values of $(w_j - k)$ for $w_j = k, k + 1, k - 1$, will be a left-shift permutation of (exp_1,exp_2,exp_3), the values of $x - k$, for $x = k - 1,k,k + 1$.

Consider now the special case where k is maximal or minimal, including the case where there are less than three elements in the discrete ordered sequence (e.g., the sequence $\{0,1\}$). The table in Figure 4.7 is used to argue the effectiveness of the selected tests for the case where k is maximal.

The tests in Figure 4.7 do not distinguish between $x < k$ and $x \neq k$, or between $x \geq k$ and $x = k$, indicating either that the tests are inadequate, or that in this situation these relations are equivalent. The latter is the case when k is the maximal discrete element: there is no distinction between the use of $<$ and $\neq$ and between $\geq$ and $=$. The tests also will not distinguish between $x \leq k$ and $w_j \leq k$ or between $x > k$ and $w_j > k$. Again, these are equivalent, since even though x and w_j are different independent variables, the outcomes

	x rel y			w_j rel y			x rel w_j		
	(0,0)	(0,1)	(1,0)	(1,0)	(0,1)	(1,0)	(0,1)	(0,0)	(1,1)
$>$	f	f	t	t	f	t	f	f	f
$\leq$	t	t	f	f	t	f	t	t	t
	(0,0)	(0,1)	(1,0)	(1,0)	(1,1)	(0,0)	(0,1)	(0,1)	(1,0)
$<$	f	t	f	f	f	f	t	t	f
$\geq$	t	f	t	t	t	t	f	f	t
$=$	t	f	f	f	t	t	f	f	f
$\neq$	f	t	t	t	f	f	t	t	t

FIGURE 4.6. Values of two variable relations for {0,1} domain.

for $x \leq k$ and $w_j \leq k$ will both always be true and, for $x > k$ and $w_j > k$, always false.

For the case where k is minimal, the argument is similar. This implies that the tests $(x,w_j) = (0,1),(1,0)$ form an effective equivalence procedure in the case where the relational function is x *rel* 0 or x *rel* 1.

4.7.3 Systems of Relations

The construction of equivalence procedures for systems of relations is a very complicated problem and is, in general, unsolvable. There is no effective method which can be used to determine the equivalence of two arbitrary systems of arithmetic relations. Fortunately, the systems of relations which occur along many paths through a program are very simple. Several simple cases are described in this section. The first involves independent relations.

Suppose that f is the function formed from the following system of relations

$$f_1 \text{ and } f_2 \text{ and } f_3 \text{ and } \dots \text{ and } f_n.$$

Then f is a *conjunctive* system of relations. If all of the and logical operators are changed to or operators, then f is a *disjunctive* system. A system of relations is *independent* if no two relations have variables in common, and if all

	x rel k		w_j rel k	
	$(k - 1, k)$	(k, k)	(k, k)	$(k - 1, k)$
$<$	t	f	f	t
$\leq$	t	t	t	t
$>$	f	f	f	f
$\geq$	f	t	t	f
$=$	f	t	t	f
$\neq$	t	f	f	t

FIGURE 4.7. Test outcome for x *rel* k where k is maximal.

variables are independent of each other. The following simple theorems describe equivalence procedures for sets of conjunctive and disjunctive relations. The term *useful* equivalence testing procedure will mean an effective, partially effective, statistically effective, or statistically partially effective testing method.

Theorem 4.22. Let f be a conjunctive system of relations:

$$f = (f_1 \text{ and } f_2 \text{ and } \ldots \text{ and } f_n).$$

Let F_f be a set of functions of the form

$$f' = (f_1' \text{ and } f_2' \text{ and } \ldots \text{ and } f_n'$$

where each f_i' belongs to a set F_i having the following properties:

(i) f_i is in F_i,
(ii) there is a useful testing procedure for F_i.

Furthermore, assume that for each f' in F_f, $f_i' = f_i$ except for at most one i, $1 \le i \le n$. Let T_i be the test set for F_i and suppose it is possible to extend each test t in T_i to a test u which is the same as t for the variables in f_i, but which contains values for all other variables also, and has the property that when f is evaluated at u, where u is derived from a test t in T_i, each f_j will evaluate to true for $j \ne i$. Let U_i be the set of tests of f which is formed by extending the tests t in T_i and let U be the set of all tests in all U_i, $1 \le i \le n$. Then U is an equivalence test set for F_f.

Proof. Let f' be in F_f. By construction, f' is a conjunction of n terms f_i' and differs from f in at most one term k. Consider f_k. The testing of f and f' over U will result in the testing of f_k and f_k' over T_k. If f_k and f_k' are not equivalent then on at least one test t in T_k, $f_k(t) \ne f_k'(t)$. Let u be the test in U formed by augmenting t with values for the other variables in the other terms. By construction, all other terms f_i, $i \ne k$, will evaluate to true when f and f' are evaluated at u. This implies that f will evaluate either to a conjunction of all true terms with one false term and f' to a conjunction of all true terms, or f will evaluate to a conjunction of all true terms and f' to a conjunction of all true terms with one false term. Hence $f(u) \ne f'(u)$.

The following theorem is the disjunctive analogue of Theorem 4.22.

Theorem 4.23. Let f be a disjunctive system of relations:

$$f = (f_1 \text{ or } f_2 \text{ or } \ldots \text{ or } f_n).$$

Let F_f be a set of relational functions of the form described in Theorem 4.22. Construct the test set U as in that theorem except extend the tests t to tests u which cause all the disjunctive terms except f_i, the term under consideration, to evaluate to false. Then U is an equivalence-determining test.

Proof. The proof is similar to that for Theorem 4.22 except in this case it depends on the fact that if two disjunctive expressions are such that all of their terms evaluate to false except for two corresponding terms which evaluate to different values (one to true and one to false), then the disjunctive expressions will evaluate to different values.

Independent systems of relations are one kind of simple system. Another is a reducible system. A *reducible system* is one which is equivalent to a single relation. A nonindependent system may be reduced to an independent one if all the sets of dependent relations form reducible subsystems. This commonly occurs in programming.

Theorem 4.24. Suppose that f is a conjunctive system of relations

$$x \ rel_1 \ y \text{ and } x \ rel_2 \ y \text{ and } \ldots \text{ and } x \ rel_n \ y$$

where *rel* is either $<, \leq, >, \geq, =,$ or $\neq$. Then f is equivalent to a single relation of the same form or is universally false, that is, always evaluates to false.

Proof. It is only necessary to show that each pair of such relations reduces to a single relation and a conjunction having more terms can be reduced one term at a time. Figure 4.8 (see pg. 72) contains a reduction table for conjunctive pairs of relations. Each entry in the table corresponds to the two-term conjunctive system of relations ($x \ rel_1 \ y$ and $x \ rel_2 \ y$) where rel_1 and rel_2 are one of the arithmetic relations. The entry in the table shows the single term $x \ rel \ y$ to which ($x \ rel_1 \ y$ and $x \ rel_2 \ y$) is equivalent. The table indicates, for example, that ($x \ rel_1 \ y$ and $x \ rel_2 \ y$), for rel_1 equal to $>$ and rel_2 equal to $\geq$, is logically equivalent to $x > y$.

A similar theorem can be proved for disjunctive systems of relations.

Theorem 4.25. Suppose that f is a disjunctive system of relations

$$x \ rel_1 \ y \text{ or } x \ rel_2 \ y \text{ or } \ldots \text{ or } x \ rel_n \ y$$

where *rel* is either $<, \leq, >, \geq, =,$ or $\neq$. Then f is equivalent to a single relation of the same form or is universally true.

Proof. Consider the reduction table in Figure 4.9 (see pg. 72).

In addition to independent and reducible systems there are systems in which relations share variables, but can often still be treated independently. Consider the systems of the form

$$x \ rel_1 \ y_1 \text{ and } x \ rel_2 \ y_2 \text{ and} \ldots \text{ and } x \ rel_n \ y_n$$

and

$$x \ rel_1 \ y_1 \text{ or } x \ rel_2 \ y_2 \text{ or } \ldots \text{ or } x \ rel_n \ y_n$$

where $rel_i = <, \leq, >, \geq, =,$ or $\neq$. Assume that the y_i are independent variables. The first form is a *half-dependent conjunctive system* of relations

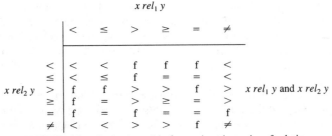
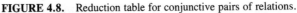

FIGURE 4.8.   Reduction table for conjunctive pairs of relations.

and the second, a *half-dependent disjunctive system*. There is a very wide range of situations under which equivalence procedures for independent systems can be used for these systems.

Recall that the basic procedure for independent systems was to test each relation individually by forcing all other relations to true or false (for conjunction and disjunction) while examining that individual relation over an equivalence-determining set of tests. The following theorems indicate how this procedure can also be done for half-dependent systems.

Theorem 4.26. Suppose that f is a half-dependent relational function of the form

$$x \, rel_1 \, y_1 \text{ and } x \, rel_2 \, y_2 \text{ and} \ldots \text{ and } x \, rel_n \, y_n$$

and let F_f be the set of all functions which can be generated from f by changing a single relation rel_i to some other relation rel_i' or by changing some variable y_i to another variable y_i', where $y_i' = y_j$ for some j, $1 \le j \le n$, or $y_i = w_j$, where w_j, $1 \le j \le m$, is an additional set of variables. Note that x remains unaltered. Suppose that all variables take on their values in a discrete ordered set with at least four elements. Assume $(d - 1, d, d + 1, d + 2)$ are elements in the ordered set. Then the following effective procedure can be used to test the equivalence of f with any f' in F_f. For each k, $1 \le k \le n$, construct the following three tests.

FIGURE 4.9.   Reduction table for disjunctive pairs of relations.

(i) $x = d, d, d + 1$ (first, second, and third tests)

(ii) $y_k = d + 1, d, d$ (first, second, and third tests)

(iii) $w_j = d - 1$ (or $d + 2$) for all three tests, $1 \le j \le m$,

(iv) y_j, for $j \ne k$, is assigned different values for each of the three tests, and the value depends on the relation rel_j occurring in $x\ rel_j y_j$. The three values are defined in the table in Figure 4.10.

Proof. Suppose f' is selected from F_f. Now f and f' are of the form

$$x\ rel_1\ y_1 \text{ and } x\ rel_2\ y_2 \text{ and} \ldots \text{ and } x\ rel_n\ y_n$$

and

$$x\ rel_1'\ y_1' \text{ and } x\ rel_2'\ y_2' \text{ and} \ldots \text{ and } x\ rel_n' y_n'$$

and f and f' differ in at most one term, say term k. Consider the tests. If $x\ rel_k\ y_k$ differs from $x\ rel_k'\ y_k'$, then either $rel_k \ne rel_k'$ or $y_k \ne y_k'$. In the case where $rel_k \ne rel_k'$, $x\ rel_k\ y_k$ will be tested against $x\ rel_k'\ y_k$ over $(d, d + 1)$, (d, d), and $(d + 1, d)$. Regardless of what rel_k is, the fact that $rel_k \ne rel_k'$ implies that these two relations will give different outcomes on at least one test. This follows directly from Theorem 4.17, since $(x - y_k)$ will be $(-1, 0, 1)$.

Alternatively, suppose $rel_k = rel_k'$ but $y_k \ne y_k'$. This implies that either $y_k' = w_j$ for some j, $1 \le j \le m$, or $y_k' = y_j$ for some $j \ne k$. Consider the first case. Since w_j is $d - 1$ (or $d + 2$), $x\ rel_k'\ y_k'$ will get tested over $(d, d - 1)$, $(d, d - 1)$, and $(d + 1, d - 1)$. The outcome will either be true on all three tests or false on all three tests. On at least one of the tests $(d, d + 1)$, (d, d), and $(d + 1, d)$, $x\ rel_k\ y_k$ will give a true value and on at least one test a false value so that $x\ rel_k\ y_k$ and $x\ rel_k'\ y_k'$ will return different values on at least one test. Suppose that $y_k' = y_j$ where $j \ne k$. In this case, $x\ rel_k'\ y_k' = x\ rel_k\ y_i$ will always evaluate to true for each of the three tests defined above. Consequently, $x\ rel_k\ y_k$ and $x\ rel_k\ y_k' = x\ rel_k\ y_i$ will evaluate differently on at least one test.

Hence, whatever the way in which they differ, $x\ rel_k\ y_k$ and $x\ rel_k'\ y_k'$ will have different outcomes on at least one of the prescribed tests. Also, $x\ rel_j\ y_j$ will always evaluate to true for $j \ne k$. It therefore follows from Theorem 4.22 that the tests are effective for determining the equivalence of f with any f' in F_f.

A similar theorem can be proved for half-dependent disjunctive relations.

$$y_j$$

<	$d + 2$	$d + 2$	$d + 2$
≤	$d + 2$	$d + 2$	$d + 2$
>	$d - 1$	$d - 1$	$d - 1$
≥	$d - 1$	$d - 1$	$d - 1$
=	d	d	$d + 1$
≠	$d + 2$	$d + 2$	$d + 2$

FIGURE 4.10. y_j values for half-dependent conjunctive system of relations.

Theorem 4.27. Suppose that f is a half-dependent relational system of the form

$$x\ rel_1\ y_1\ \text{or}\ x\ rel_2\ y_2\ \text{or}\ldots\ \text{or}\ x\ rel_n\ y_n$$

and let F_f be defined as in Theorem 4.25. The following $3n$ tests are effective for determining the equivalence of f with any f' in F_f. For each k, $1 \le k \le n$, construct the following tests:

- **(i)** $x = d,d,d + 1$ (first, second, and third tests),
- **(ii)** $y_k = d + 1,d,d$ (first, second, and third tests),
- **(iii)** $w_j = d - 1$ (or $d + 2$) for all three tests, $1 \le j \le m$, and
- **(iv)** y_j, for $j \ne k$, is assigned different values for the three tests, and the value depends on the relation rel_j in $x\ rel_j\ y_j$. The values are defined in the table in Figure 4.11.

The proof is similar to that of Theorem 4.26.

Theorems 4.24 and 4.25 can be used to determine if a system of relations of the form

$$x\ rel_1\ y\ \text{and}\ x\ rel_2\ y\ldots\ \text{and}\ x\ rel_n\ y$$

or

$$x\ rel_1\ y\ \text{or}\ x\ rel_2\ y\ldots\ \text{or}\ x\ rel_n\ y$$

has a solution (i.e., is feasible). Another class of systems for which there are also simple feasibility rules is described as follows.

Theorem 4.28. Suppose that f is a conjunctive system of relations of the form

$$x\ rel_1\ k_1\ \text{and}\ x\ rel_2\ k_2\ \text{and}\ldots\ \text{and}\ x\ rel_n\ k_n$$

where rel_i is $<$, $\le$, $>$, $\ge$, $=$, or $\ne$ and k_i is a constant. Then the feasibility of f (i.e., whether or not it is equivalent to false) can be determined using the following rules.

- **(i)** If there is more than one relation of the form $x = k_i$, then unless the constants in all such relations are the same, the system has no solution. Assume there is only one such relation.

		y_j		
	$<$	$d - 1$	$d - 1$	$d - 1$
	$\le$	$d - 1$	$d - 1$	$d - 1$
	$>$	$d + 2$	$d + 2$	$d + 2$
rel_j	$\ge$	$d + 2$	$d + 2$	$d + 2$
	$=$	$d + 2$	$d + 2$	$d + 2$
	$\ne$	d	d	$d + 1$

FIGURE 4.11. y_j values for half-dependent disjunctive system of relations.

(ii) For all relations of the form $x \leq k_i$ or $x > k_i$, choose the one with the minimal constant and discard the others. For all of the form $x \geq k_i$ or $x > k_i$ choose the one with the maximal constant and discard the others.

(iii) Assume that the system has at most one relation of the form $x \geq k_1$, or $x > k_1$, one relation of the form $x = k_2$, and one of the form $x \leq k_3$ or $x < k_3$. It may have one or more relations of the form $x \neq k_4$. The feasibility of the system of relations can be determined using the table in Figure 4.12. It describes each of the different possibilities and the condition necessary for feasibility. The part of the condition involving k_4 is relevant only if there is an inequality in the system. If there is more than one such inequality it must hold for all such inequalities.

The development of effective equivalence rules for discrete relations is a new area of exploration. Research into patterns of relations that commonly occur in actual programs can be expected to continue, resulting in the development of additional equivalence procedures.

4.8 FLOW-GRAPH STRUCTURES

Functions, states, and type transformations are joined together into directed graph structures. Structural analysis involves the traversal of paths through the graphs, and the analysis of the interconnections and interfaces that occur along paths. All structures will be assumed to be a special kind of directed graph called a flow graph.

A *flow graph* is a set of *arcs* and *nodes* such that each arc connects one node to another. The arcs are directed. There is one *start node* in the graph, a node which has an arc coming out of it but no arc going into it. There are one or more *terminal nodes*, nodes which have arcs coming into them but no arcs coming out. Two nodes may be connected by more than one arc. Each arc and/or node may have a *label*. The labels need not be different. A *path* through a graph is a connected sequence of nodes and arcs of the form

	relations			*condition*	
$k_1 \leq x$	$x = k_2$	$x \leq k_3$	$k_1 \leq k_2 \leq k_3$	$k_2 \neq k_4$
$k_1 < x$	$x = k_2$	$x \leq k_3$	$k_1 < k_2 \leq k_3$	$k_2 \neq k_4$
$k_1 \leq x$	$x = k_2$	$x < k_3$	$k_1 \leq k_2 < k_3$	$k_2 \neq k_4$
$k_1 < x$	$x = k_2$	$x < k_3$	$k_1 < k_2 < k_3$	$k_2 \neq k_4$
$k_1 \leq x$	$x = k_2$		$k_1 \leq k_2$	$k_2 \neq k_4$
$k_1 < x$	$x = k_2$		$k_1 < k_2$	$k_2 \neq k_4$
$k_1 \leq x$		$x \leq k_3$	$k_1 \leq k_3$	$\{if\ k_1 = k_3$
$k_1 < x$		$x \leq k_3$	$k_1 < k_3$	$then\ k_1 \neq k_4\}$
$k_1 \leq x$		$x < k_3$	$k_1 < k_3$	
$k_1 < x$		$x < k_3$	$k_1 < k_3$	
	$x = k_2$	$x < k_3$	$k_2 < k_3$	$k_2 \neq k_4$
	$x = k_2$	$x \leq k_3$	$k_2 \leq k_3$	$k_2 \neq k_4$

FIGURE 4.12. Feasibility conditions for simple conjunctive system of relations.

$n_0 a_1 n_1 a_2 n_2 \ldots a_k n_k$ where n_i is a node, a_i is an arc, and the arc a_i goes from node n_{i-1} to node n_i. A complete path through the graph starts from the start node and ends at a terminal node. Flow graphs have the property that for each node n in the graph, there is a path from the start node to n and a path from n to a terminal node. A flow graph is *acyclic* if it does not contain a path which starts and ends at the same node.

In some applications it is important to know when one graph is a *subgraph* of another. Suppose that F and G are two flow graphs whose nodes and arcs may be labeled. Then F is a subgraph of G if there is a mapping h from all the nodes and arcs of F to nodes and arcs in G which has the following properties.

(i) If a node n in F is labeled, then $h(n)$, the node in G which h maps n on to, has the same label as n.

(ii) If two nodes n_1 and n_2 in F are connected by an arc a from n_1 to n_2, then $h(n_1)$ is connected to $h(n_2)$ by $h(a)$.

(iii) If an arc a in F is labeled, then $h(a)$ has the same label as a.

The term path will sometimes, when obvious, be taken to mean the sequence of node and/or arc labels that occur along a path. Two paths are *equivalent* if they have the same sequence of labels. They are *distinct* if they are not equivalent. Two graphs are equivalent if every path in either graph is equivalent to some path in the other.

The theoretical results used in structural analysis are of two kinds. The first proves coverage properties for path traversal algorithms. They prove that all of certain specified parts of a graph will be visited when certain graph traversal algorithms are used. The second consists of graph equivalence algorithms which prove equivalence relationships between graphs.

The first two theorems prove that all of a graph's nodes and node pairs are included in simple subsets of a graph's paths.

Theorem 4.29. Suppose that G is a flow graph and let p_i, $1 \le i \le m$, be the set of all paths through G which do not traverse the same node more than twice. Then for every node or arc there is at least one path p_k which contains that node or arc.

Proof. Suppose n is a node in G. Let p' be the shortest path from the start node to n (i.e., has the smallest number of nodes) and let p'' be the shortest path from n to a terminal node. Such paths exist by definition of a flow graph. Let p be the path constructed by joining p' and p''. Now p' does not have any repeated nodes. If it did, then the path segment from the first occurrence of that node to its repetition could be deleted, and the result would be a path from the start node to n which was shorter than p'. Similarly p'' does not have any repeated nodes.

Consider p. If it has repeated nodes, it is because the same node occurs in both p' and p''. However since such a node could appear at most once in p' and p'', it occurs at most twice in p. Hence there is a path from the start node to a terminal node which passes through n and which contains no node more than twice, so that the set of all paths which traverse no node more than twice contains each node in at least one path.

Similar arguments can be used to prove that the set of all such paths includes all arcs in the flow graph.

Theorem 4.30. Suppose that G is a flow graph and let n_1 and n_2 be two nodes such that there is a subpath s from n_1 to n_2 in G. Let p_i, $1 \leq i \leq m$, be the set of all paths through G which do not traverse the same node more than three times. Then there is at least one path p_i which contains both n_1 and n_2 and which has a subpath s' which goes from n_1 to n_2.

Proof. Let p_1 be the shortest path from the start node to n_1. As in Theorem 4.29 it can be assumed that p_1 does not contain any node more than once. Similarly, let p_2 be the shortest path from n_2 to a terminal node. Let s' be the shortest path from n_1 to n_2. Such a path exists because of the existence of the subpath s. Again, s' will contain no node more than once. Hence the path which can be constructed by joining p_1, s', and p_2 can contain no node more than three times, once each for p_1, s', and p_2, and hence there is a path through G which contains n_1 and n_2 and which contains no node more than three times.

The paths in Theorem 4.29, the set of all paths which traverse no node more than twice, will be referred to as the $r(2)$ (repetition at most twice) *paths*. Those that traverse a node no more than three times are the $r(3)$ *paths* and those which traverse a node at most once, the $r(1)$ *paths*.

The paths in Theorems 4.29 and 4.30 can be generated using a modified depth-first graph traversal process which terminates either when a graph terminal node is reached or when a node is encountered for the third or fourth time.

To carry out the depth-first traversal of graph G, a stack s is used to keep track of multiple branching nodes in G and which branches have been followed from those nodes. Each time a new node is considered, if it has more than one branch from it, one of these is selected. The node, along with the identity of the followed branch, is pushed on the traversal stack. If there is only one branch, no stacking is done and the branch is followed. If there is no branch out of the node, a terminal node has been reached and the traversal process backs up by popping the stack. Suppose x is an element that has been popped off the stack and n is the node associated with x. Choose one of the branches from n which are not identified in x as having been already followed, alter x to record that this additional branch has now been followed, and if there are more unfollowed branches push x back on the stack.

Follow the selected branch. If there are no more elements on the stack, the traversal terminates.

This process will not terminate for a flow graph that contains a loop since it will continue to push elements for the loop nodes on the stack indefinitely. The modifications of the depth-first traversal process needed to cover all $r(1)$, $r(2)$, and $r(3)$ paths involve the introduction of a loop termination condition into the traversal process. Associate a counter with each node in the graph. Each time a new node is to be considered its counter is examined. If the counter has reached its limit value, the procedure acts as though a terminal node has been encountered and backs up. Otherwise the counter is incremented and the depth-first traversal continues normally. Stacking and backing up are the same as in the unmodified depth-first traversal procedure.

The $r(2)$ and $r(3)$ path coverage traversals of a graph are very expensive in the sense that their operating times are potentially exponential relative to the number of nodes in a graph. This is because the number of $r(2)$ or $r(3)$ paths through a graph containing n nodes can be exponential in n. If it is necessary to look at *all* paths "up to iterations" through a graph, then this cannot be avoided. Fortunately, in structural analysis it is often only necessary to generate node pair interfaces in a graph and not paths, and this can be done more efficiently. The following *np* (node pair) modification of depth-first traversal will accomplish this.

A node pair interface is a pair of nodes (n_1, n_2) that are connected by an arc from n_1 to n_2. The set of all node pairs in a graph can be generated using a version of the depth-first algorithm which traverses all $r(1)$ paths and which is modified to generate a node pair whenever one is discovered. In this version of depth-first traversal, called *np traversal* (node-pair traversal), each node has associated with it a "visited" flag and an unfollowed branches list. All flags are initially set to not-visited. The first time a node is reached a number of operations are carried out. The first is to set its flag to visited so that the traverser will know the node has been previously reached the next time it encounters it. If the node has only one branch coming out of it this is followed. If there is more than one branch, one is followed and the rest are put in the unfollowed branches list for the node and the node is pushed on the node stack. The second and subsequent times the node is reached, the traverser terminates the path and backs up by popping the node stack. Suppose n is a node popped off the stack. The traverser gets a branch from the unfollowed branch list for n, and deletes this entry from the list. If the list is still nonempty, then the identifier for the node is pushed back on the node stack. The traverser also backs up when it reaches a terminal node. When it is not possible to do any backing up, the traverser terminates. Each time the traverser follows a branch it produces the node pair associated with the branch.

The following theorems prove the efficiency of np traversal, and prove that it will generate all node pairs.

Theorem 4.31. Suppose that k is the maximal number of edges between any pair of nodes. The np traversal process will examine less than kn^2 nodes in its traversal of a graph containing n nodes.

Proof. The traverser follows no branch more than once. Hence the maximum number of times a node can be reached is equal to the number of branches coming into it. This has to be less than kn so that at most kn^2 node encounters occur during traversal.

It remains to show that all node pairs, that is, graph edges, will be traversed by this procedure.

Theorem 4.32. The np traverser will traverse every graph edge and hence can be used to produce all node pairs in a flow graph.

Proof. Clearly all branches from the starting node will be followed. Suppose some edge e, joining nodes n_1 and n_2 is not followed. Choose an edge such that a branch coming into n_1 is traversed. This is possible since every branch from the start node is followed and there must be some "first" unfollowed branch. But by construction of the traversal process, e must be followed when n_1 is first reached or later on when n_1 is popped off the node stack.

A related situation occurs when it is necessary to examine label-pair interfaces rather than node-pair interfaces. Suppose that some or all of the nodes in a graph G have labels. A *label-pair* interface is a pair of labels (a,b) from a node pair (n_1, n_2) that has the property that there is a subpath in G from n_1 to n_2 which contains no other labeled nodes. Two nodes may have the same label.

It is more complex to efficiently produce all possible *different* label-pair interfaces for a graph than it is to produce simple node pairs. Two label pairs are different if they have different first and/or second labels. If the same label pair can be produced from different pairs of nodes, due to labeling different nodes with the same labels, it is not necessary to produce the label pair more than once. The following modification of depth-first traversal, called lp traversal (label-pair traversal), can be used to produce all different label pairs.

The algorithm associates a *previous label set* with each node. There is one such set for each node and like the visited flag in the node-pair traverser, it is not stacked during the depth-first traversal process. In addition, there is also a current label, which is stacked. Initially, all previous label sets are empty and there is no current label. The procedure begins with the start node. If it has a label, this becomes the current label, and a branch is selected from the branches leading out of the start node. If there is more than one such branch, the start node is stacked along with a record of which branches were not followed, and also with the identity of the current label.

When a node is reached after traversing a branch, the previous label set for the node is examined to see if it contains the current label. If so, path termination occurs and the traversal stack is popped. If not, the current label is added to the node's previous label set. If the node has a label this becomes the new current label. A branch out of the node is then selected and stacking carried out if there is more than one branch.

The use of a dummy node label is used to take care of the situation when control arrives at a node with no current label. If the dummy label is in the previous label set, the traverser knows that this has previously occurred and terminates the path. If the dummy label is not in the previous label set when control arrives with no current label, a dummy label is put in the set. The situation where there is no current label occurs when the start node is not labeled.

During backing up, a stack entry is popped to find a node from which to continue the traversal process. When the node is popped, an associated current label and list of unfollowed branches is popped along with it. One of the remaining branches in the unfollowed branches list is selected, the branch list updated, the node and associated information restacked, and traversal initiated along the selected branch with the popped current label for the node.

The label-pair algorithm will produce a label-pair interface each time it reaches a node having a label for which it does not do a path termination. The pair will be the current label and this new label.

In lp traversal when a node is stacked, so are a current label and a list of branches that have not yet been followed from the node. This is because it is necessary to traverse the same branch from a node more than once if the branch can be followed with different current labels. The list of unfollowed branches is not stacked in np traversal since no branch is ever followed more than once.

The validity of the label-pair traversal algorithm is argued in the following theorem.

Theorem 4.33. Suppose that n_1 and n_2 are two nodes in a flow graph having labels a and b and that there is a subpath from n_1 to n_2 which contains no labeled nodes. Then the lp-traversal algorithm will encounter and produce the label pair (a,b).

Proof. The proof depends on the observation that every edge in the flow graph will be traversed at least once during lp traversal. This can be proved as follows. Suppose e is a flow-graph edge from node m_1 to node m_2. There will, by definition of a flow graph, be a path p from the start node to m_1, and then from m_1 to m_2 along arc e. Suppose that e is not traversed. Then go backwards along p towards the start node to find the last arc in p which is traversed. Suppose it is an arc e_k from m_k to m_{k+1}. When the lp traverser reaches m_{k+1} if it does not terminate it will traverse, either now or later after backup, all arcs leading out of m_{k+1}, including arc e_{k+1}, the next arc in p. If it terminates it is because m_{k+1} was previously encountered with the same current label as this encounter. After the first of such encounters with m_{k+1}, the lp traverser will have gone out all arcs from m_{k+1}, as above. Hence arc e_{k+1} from m_{k+1} is traversed, contrary to the assertion that arc e_k is the last arc in p which is traversed. The only other possibility is that there is no last arc in p which was traversed, since none of them are. But this would mean that some arc out of the start node is not traversed, contradicting the way that lp traversal is defined. Hence all edges are traversed at least once.

Suppose that e is an edge from m_1 to m_2 and that m_1 is labeled. Then e will be traversed with that label whenever e is traversed, by definition of lp traversal. Suppose that m_1 is not labeled. Then e will be traversed with any of the current labels that m_1 is arrived at during traversal, the first time that m_1 is arrived at with that label.

Consider now the subpath from n_1 to n_2. Since n_1 is labeled with a, the edges out of n_1 will be traversed with current label a, including the edge in the label-free subpath from n_1 to n_2. Since the nodes in this subpath are label-free, the next edge in the subpath will also get traversed with current label a. Eventually the edge coming into n_2 will be traversed with current label a and the label pair (a,b) will be generated.

It now remains to consider the efficiency of the lp-traversal process.

Theorem 4.34. Suppose that t is the number of distinct labels in a flow graph g having n nodes. Then the lp traversal process will examine less than $(t + 1)n^2$ different nodes.

Proof. If a node is arrived at, it must be reached from a predecessor node which has a branch to that node. There are less than n such predecessors for a node. The maximum number of times such a branch will be followed is $t + 1$ due to the path-traversal termination process that takes place when a node is reached for the second time with the same current label, or for the second time with no current label. Hence each node is examined less than $(t + 1)n$ times and less than $n * (t + 1)n = (t + 1)n^2$ nodes are examined altogether.

Notice that np traversal is a special case of lp traversal. The np-traversal algorithm is more efficient because the number of times that a branch from one node to the next is traversed is exactly one since every node is labeled. A different bound on lp traversal can be given if a bound on d, the maximum number of branches that come into a node, is known. The maximum number of nodes that will be examined will be $(t + 1)dn$. In the case where t is less than 5, which is the case for some very important structural analysis problems, and where d is 4, a reasonable approximation for flow graphs for computer programs, the number of nodes examined is less than $20n$ implying that we can expect lp traversal (and hence np traversal) to be essentially linear.

In some cases it is possible to further increase the efficiency of a flow-graph traversal procedure by doing parallel analysis. Suppose that a flow graph has t labels that can be put into k disjoint sets having $t_1, t_2, \ldots, t_k$ labels each, and that it is only necessary to guarantee the production of all label pairs that are formed from labels within a single set. This can be done by carrying out the traversals for each set in parallel and if t' is the maximum value of t_i, it will result in at most $(t' + 1)\, n^2$ node examinations. The parallel-traversal process will require k previous label sets for each node and k current label identifiers. The path termination process will "cancel" current labels as termination occurs for their respective label sets. When all have been canceled, path termination occurs.

The last kind of flow-graph coverage/traversal result that will be considered is for the special situation where nodes are labeled with label operators rather than labels. Each node has a finite set of operators which act on a current label set to produce a new label set. As in the previous graph-coverage algorithms, paths are followed from node to node through the graph. In this case a current label set is carried along during the traversal process and modified by the label operators associated with the nodes that are encountered. The label operators can either add or delete a label from the label set. The goal in the traversal of a flow graph with dynamic labels is not only to visit each node at least once, but to visit each node with each possible current label set that could occur at the node during some traversal of the graph.

The *dynamic-labels* traversal algorithm (dl traversal) is again a variation of depth-first search. The traverser begins with the start node and an empty current label set. The label operators are applied to the current label set and a branch to the next node is taken. Every time a branch is followed the current label set is carried along to the next node. If a node has more than one branch, the node, a record of which branch has been followed, and the current label set are stacked. Each node has associated with it a list of previous label sets, which is used to terminate the traversal of a path. When a node is reached, the current label set which is brought along from the previous node is compared with the label sets in the previous label sets list. If it is in the list already, the path is terminated. If it is not in the list, the label operations are applied and it is added to the list. Paths are also terminated when a graph termination node is reached. When path termination occurs, an entry is popped off the stack, and backing up to a previously unfollowed branch occurs in the normal way.

Since nodes may have no label operators, or no operators which add labels to the current label set, it is necessary to allow the special case where the current label set is empty. The traverser must be able to put empty label sets in previous label set lists and compare them with current label sets in the same way as for nonempty label sets.

Theorem 4.35. Suppose G is a flow graph with label operators. The dl-traversal algorithm will visit every node in G at least once with each of the current label sets that could occur at that node during all possible path traversals of G.

Proof. Suppose p is a path in G from the start node to a node n_k, and that C is the current label set which would occur at n_k if p were followed. Let $p = n_0 e_1 n_1 e_2 \ldots n_{k-1} e_k \, n_k$. By definition of dl traversal, e_1 will be followed from n_0, and n_1 will be arrived at with the original current label set C from n_0. Either termination will occur or the label operators associated with n_1 will be applied to produce a new current label set C', and e_2 will be followed with the new current label set. This will happen either now, or later, when control returns to n_1 as the traverser backtracks using its stack. If termination occurs, it is because n_1 was previously reached with current label set C. The first time this happened the label operators would have been applied to C to produce C' and e_2 followed (either immediately, or later after backing up). Hence, during dl traversal, n_1 will be arrived at, at some point with the same current label set that it would have arrived at along p, the label operators associated with n_1 will be applied to form a new current label set C', and the branch e_2 followed out of n_1.

    The above argument can be applied inductively to prove that for all i, $1 \leq i \leq k$, the dl traverser will arrive at node n_i with the same current label set as would be constructed if p were followed from n_0 to n_k. Since p is arbitrary this proves the theorem.

It now remains to consider the efficiency of dl traversal.

Theorem 4.36. Suppose that t is the maximum number of labels that can occur in a current label set for a flow graph having n nodes. Then the dl traverser will examine less than $2^{t+1} \, n$ nodes.

Proof. The maximum number of different possible current label sets is

$$\sum_{i=0}^{t} \binom{t}{i} = 2^t.$$

This implies that each node is visited less than 2^{t+1} times.

    The exponential factor in the above formulae is not as ominous as it looks for two reasons. The first is that t is likely to be small, and secondly, in some analyses, the label operators can be divided up into disjoint sets and analyzed in parallel, as mentioned earlier for np and lp traversal.

    The following theorems prove equivalency relationships between graphs. The first describes a way of determining if the paths in one graph are equivalent to paths in a second graph. The second theorem also describes a way of proving that all paths in one graph are equivalent to paths in another.

The third theorem characterizes conditions under which one graph can be shown to be a subgraph of another.

> **Theorem 4.37.** Suppose that G is a flow graph all of whose nodes are labeled and assume that all paths in G are distinct (i.e., their label sequences are different). Suppose that G' is a flow graph which is either the same as G or can be derived from G by the insertion of a labeled node into the middle of an arc in G. Then an effective procedure for determining the equivalence of G' with G is to see if every $r(2)$ path in G is also a path in G' (i.e., the sequence of node labels that occurs along any $r(2)$ path in G also occurs in G'). If every $r(2)$ path in G is also in G', then $G = G'$. Otherwise G' differs from G by a node insertion.

> ***Proof.*** Assume that $G' \neq G$, but is one of the flow graphs that can be constructed by the insertion of a node into an arc in G, and that all $r(2)$ paths in G are also in G'. It will be shown that this leads to a contradiction.
>   Suppose that the inserted node is n and the arc in G into which it is inserted is e. The insertion of n into G results in the insertion of n into some of the paths in G, but not others depending on whether the paths contain e. Let p be the shortest path containing e. Then p is an $r(2)$ path. This is argued as follows. Suppose it were not. Then some node m must be repeated at least 3 times in p so that p can be written
>
> $$p = n_0 e_1 n_1 e_2 \ldots n_i \ldots n_j \ldots n_k \ldots e_t n_t$$
>
> where n_i, n_j and n_k are all the node m. If the arc e does not occur in either the subpath from n_i to n_j or the subpath from n_j to n_k, delete the subpath not containing it. If it occurs in both subpaths, delete either one. The result will be a shorter path in G containing e, a contradiction. Hence the shortest path p in G containing e is an $r(2)$ path.
>   Let p' be the path in G' resulting from the insertion of the node into p in G. Then p' must be the shortest path in G' containing the node. If there were a shorter path in G', then there would be a corresponding path in G which is smaller then p.
>   Now if all $r(2)$ paths in G are also in G', there must be some path in G' which is equivalent to p (i.e., has the same sequence of node labels). Consider first those paths in G' which do not contain the inserted node. It cannot be one of these, since they also occur in G and are not p so that there would be two equivalent paths in G, violating the distinctness criterion. This means that p must be equivalent to a path in G' which contains the inserted node. But p' is the shortest of these and the number of nodes in p' is at least one greater than the number of nodes in p, so that p cannot be equivalent to p' or any other path containing the inserted node. Hence there is no path in G' which is equivalent to the $r(2)$ path p and G and G' must be the same flow graph.

The next two equivalence results require that one of the graphs have special properties.

Suppose that G is a flow graph with some or all of its nodes labeled. The *immediate labeled successors* of a node m in G are the set of all labeled nodes $(n_1, n_2, \ldots, n_k)$ such that there is an arc or a label-free subpath from m to n_i. A subpath is label free if none of its nodes, except its first and last nodes, have labels. The *immediate successor labels* of a node are the labels of its immediate labeled successors. A labeled graph is a *Markov graph* if any two nodes which have the same labels have the same immediate successor labels. Intuitively, this means that it doesn't matter where you are in a graph, if the label on one node is the same as the label on another, what can "happen next" after one node is the same as what can happen next after the other. The simplest kinds of Markov graphs are those in which all labeled nodes have different labels or all labeled nodes have the same label.

A *label pair* in a graph G is a pair of labels (a,b) taken from a pair of nodes (n_1, n_2) in G such that there is a label-free subpath from n_1 to n_2. A *label path* is a sequence of labels $(a_1, a_2, \ldots, a_t)$ such that (a_i, a_{i+1}), $1 \le i \le t - 1$, is a label pair.

Theorem 4.38. Suppose that G and G' are two flow graphs, some or all of whose nodes are labeled, and that G' is a Markov graph. If all label pairs in G are also label pairs in G', then all label paths in G are also label paths in G'.

Proof. Suppose that $(n_1, n_2, \ldots, n_t)$ is the sequence of nodes corresponding to a label path $(a_1, a_2, \ldots, a_t)$ in G and that all label pairs in G are also label pairs in G'. If $(a_1, a_2, \ldots, a_t)$ is not a label path in G' then there is some maximal $k > 2$ such that $(a_1, a_2, \ldots, a_k)$ is a label path in G' but not $(a_1, a_2, \ldots, a_k, a_{k+1})$. Suppose that the label path $(a_1, a_2, \ldots, a_k)$ corresponds to the sequence of nodes $(m_1, m_2, \ldots, m_k)$ in G'. Now (a_k, a_{k+1}) is a label pair in G and hence in G' and a_k is the label of m_k. Since G' is Markov, there must be an arc from m_k to a node m_{k+1} in G' which has label a_{k+1}, which implies that $(a_1, a_2, \ldots, a_k, a_{k+1})$ is a label path in G', a contradiction. Hence all label paths in G are also label paths in G'.

The third theorem is concerned with graphs having labeled edges rather than nodes, and also involves the concept of a graph interface. Suppose that G is a graph, all of whose arcs are labeled. Let n be any node in G and suppose the labels on its input and output arcs are $(a_1, a_2, \ldots, a_s)$ and $(b_1, b_2, \ldots, b_t)$. Then $((a_1, a_2, \ldots, a_s), (b_1, b_2, \ldots, b_t))$ is an *interface* in G.

Suppose that G is a graph all of whose edges are labeled. Then G has *completely duplicated labels* if it has the following property. Suppose that there is an arc e from n_1 to n_2 with label a and an arc t from m_1 to m_2 with label a. Then there is an arc from n_1 to m_2 with label a and an arc from m_1 to n_2 with label a. Intuitively, this means that when a label is produced by a node (i.e., it labels one of its output edges), it is made available to all nodes which use that label (i.e., nodes which have an input edge with that label).

Also, if a label is used by a node (i.e., it labels one of its input edges), then it can use all instances of the production of that label by a node (i.e., by nodes with an output edge having that label).

> **Theorem 4.39.** Suppose that G and G' are two flow graphs with labeled arcs and suppose that G' has completely duplicated labels. If all of the interfaces in G are also in G' then G is a subgraph of G'.

> **Proof.** Construct a map h from the nodes and arcs of G to those of G' as follows. Let x be an interface in G. Then there is an identical interface y in G'. Let m and n be the nodes associated with x and y in G and G' and define h so that it maps m to n.
>   Suppose that m_1 and m_2 are two nodes in G and are joined by an arc d having the label a. Let x_1 and x_2 be the interfaces in G for m_1 and m_2 and y_1 and y_2 be corresponding interfaces in G'. Let n_1 and n_2 be the nodes which h maps m_1 and m_2 on to. Since y_1 and y_2 are the same as x_1 and x_2, there is an arc e_1 from n_1 with label a and an arc e_2 into n_2 with label a. Since G' has completely duplicated labels, this means there must be an arc e from n_1 to n_2 with label a. Let h map d on to this arc e. Hence a map h can be defined which satisfies all the necessary conditions described in Section 4.8 for G to be a subgraph of G'.

4.9 SUMMARY

It can be proved that there is no general purpose, automatable procedure for deciding if a program is correct. This follows directly from results in the theory of computation. If there were such a procedure, it would then be possible to solve the well-known unsolvable halting problem.

Despite the theoretical limitations of validation, it is still possible to construct an effective, systematic approach to testing. In functional testing and analysis a program is viewed as consisting of collections of input-output functions which are arranged into structures. The functions may be overlapping and correspond to small or large parts of a program. The structures are directed graphs, and define sequences of state and type changing transformations.

Functional testing involves the analysis of the input-output behavior of individual functions. Effective testing methods are defined which can be used to detect different classes of functional faults. It is assumed that an input-output oracle is available which can be used to detect whether the output for a function on a given input is correct. In functional testing, classes of faults are defined in terms of the way in which a function is constructed from more elementary functions. Faults can be expression, conditional selection, or iteration faults. The theory of functional testing consists of proofs that when two functions in a specified class of functions agree on a certain set of input tests, then they are functionally equivalent and will agree on all inputs.

Functional or structural analysis is primarily a failure-analysis method. A failure occurs in a functional structure if an incorrect sequence of state or type changes occurs when paths through the structure are followed. Structural analysis involves techniques for determining if traversing the functional paths in a given structure will result in sequence failures. It depends on the availability of a state or type sequence oracle. This can take the form of a legal-sequences diagram. A path through a functional structure does not have a sequence failure if it corresponds to a state or type sequence which is also in the legal-sequences diagram. The theory of structural analysis consists of proofs of the effectiveness of graph-traversal algorithms for looking at all parts of a structural graph, and of the characterization of conditions under which two graphs are either equivalent or one is a subgraph of the other.

In the case where a program is to be viewed as a black box and no knowledge of its internal functions or structure is assumed, statistical results can be used to establish confidence levels for the program's correctness. A variation on hypothesis testing can be used. Suppose that θ is the probability of a program giving incorrect output when it is in production use and suppose that it has operated correctly over $h\log(h)$ tests. Then the probability of the hypothesis "$\theta < 1/h$" being incorrect is less than $1/h$.

EXERCISES

4.1. Alter Theorem 4.3 as suggested in Section 4.4 to find an optimal value t' to use in the hypothesis acceptance criteria. Using $t < t'$ (number of failures in n tests) as the acceptance criteria should reduce the probability of the type 1 error to a minimum while still keeping the probability of the type 2 error below $1/h$.

4.2. Using the inequality

$$(1 - x^{-1})^x < e^{-1}$$

prove that

$$h\log(h) > \log(h)/(\log(h) - \log(h - 1)),$$

hence allowing the simpler expression to be used for choosing test sizes in Theorem 4.3.

4.3. The results in Section 4.2 prove that there is no mechanical (i.e., programmable) procedure for determining the equivalence of any two programs p and q. The results in Sections 4.5 through 4.7 prove that equivalence proving is mechanizable for restricted classes of functions. Some classes correspond to expressions involving a particular set of operators (e.g., the arithmetic operators) and having a bounded complexity (e.g., maximum exponent). Other classes are defined in terms of a given program. A class of this kind contains the program, plus all other programs that are minor deviations from that program (e.g., expressions that differ by an additive constant). List the classes of functions described in those sections and the equivalence-determining procedures available for them. Similar classes and equivalence procedures for expressions involving nonarithmetic operations can also be developed. Construct an equivalence procedure for classes of expressions involving the simple list operations *head* (get first element), *rest* (get all but first element), and *join* (join two lists to make a new list), and which consist of all expressions that can be constructed from the composition of less than or equal to k such operations for some fixed k.

4.4. Construct equivalence procedures for half-dependent disjunctive and conjunctive discrete systems of relations of the form

$$x \ rel \ k \ \text{and} \ y \ rel \ k \ \text{and} \ \dots \ \text{and} \ z \ rel \ k$$

where k is a constant. Consider the cases where k is maximal or minimal.

4.5. Either find a counter-example showing it cannot be done, or construct an equivalence procedure for sets of flow graphs that result from the insertion of two nodes into two arcs in a graph.

4.6. Construct flow-graph equivalence procedures for graphs that have more than one start node.

REFERENCES

1. W. E. Howden, The theory and practice of functional testing, *Software*, vol. 2, 5, 1985.
2. W. E. Howden, Proving correctness by testing, *UCSD Computer Science Technical Report*, 1974.
3. T. A. Budd, R. A. DeMillo, R. J. Lipton, and F. G. Sayward, The design of a prototype mutation system for program testing, *Proceedings NCC 1978*, AFIPS, Alexandria, Va., 1978.
4. W. E. Howden, Applicability of software validation techniques to scientific programs, *ACM Transactions on Programming Languages and Systems*, 2, 1980.
5. W. E. Howden, Errors, design properties and functional program tests, in *Computer Program Testing*, in B. Chandrasakaren and S. Radicchi (Eds.), North Holland, Amsterdam, 1981.
6. L. G. Valiant, A theory of the learnable, *CACM*, vol. 27,11, 1984.
7. W. E. Howden, Algebraic equivalence of elementary computational structures, *University of Victoria Mathematics Technical Report 214*, 1980.
8. R. A. DeMillo and R. J. Lipton, A probabilistic remark on algebraic program testing, *Information Processing Letters*, 7, 1978.
9. M. Brooks, Determining correctness by testing, *Stanford University Computer Science Technical Report 80-804*, 1980.
10. T. A. Budd, R. A. DeMillo, R. J. Lipton, and F. G. Sayward, Theoretical and empirical studies on using program mutation to test the functional correctness of programs, *Proceedings ACM Symposium on Principles of Programming Languages*, Las Vegas, 1980.
11. W. E. Howden, Weak mutation testing and completeness of program test sets, *IEEE Transactions on Software Engineering*, SE-8, 1982.
12. K. A. Foster, Error sensitive test case analysis, *IEEE Transactions on Software Engineering*, SE-6, 1980.
13. K. A. Foster, Sensitive test data for logic expressions, *ACM Software Engineering Notes*, vol. 9, 2, 1984.

CHAPTER
5

FUNCTIONAL PROGRAM TESTING

5.1 INTRODUCTION

Ideally, there would be a one-to-one correspondence between program testing methods and theoretical results which could be used to establish the effectiveness of the methods. This is not the case for a number of reasons. One is that testing is a field in which much additional research needs to be done. Another is the gap between what can be done in practice and what can be proved. The material in this chapter is a mixture of conventional pragmatic testing methods and newer methods based on the theory of functional testing. In the case of the older conventional methods, their relationship to functional testing is discussed and it will be seen that they can be interpreted as approximations to functional testing. Functional testing and its theory indicate the way in which these techniques can be refined.

The testing methods which are described in the following sections depend on input-output oracles. They involve the familiar three-step procedure:

1. select test data,
2. execute program, and
3. examine output.

This is the procedure followed for functions formed by expression, conditional, or iterative synthesis. It is also the one followed for black-box functional testing. The procedure followed for functions formed by structural synthesis is somewhat different. It may not even include program execution and is discussed in the following chapter.

The first section discusses the application of statistical testing to black-box testing. This is followed by a discussion of traditional control-flow coverage metrics and their relationship to functional testing. Data-flow coverage methods are discussed, and then symbolic evaluation and its uses in infeasible path detection and automated test data generation. This is followed by a discussion of test output oracles.

5.2   BLACK-BOX TESTING

Suppose that f is the black-box function in Figure 5.1. If nothing is known about its internal structure or the class of functions to which it belongs, then statistical testing may be the only possible method for testing f.

The principal difficulty in the application of statistical testing is the need to know a program's *operational input distribution*. This is the frequency with which different inputs to a program are selected during actual use of the program. A program is either correct or not correct, so that it does not make any sense to talk about the probability of a program being correct. All that can be done is to discuss the probability of selecting a point from its input domain on which the program is correct, and this is only meaningful if input data is selected according to the operational distribution for the program.

If no model for a program's operational input distribution can be constructed, then the only alternative may be to put a program or system into trial use. This will result in its being tested over its operational distribution. Suppose that θ is the probability that the program will operate incorrectly in production use. The statistical results of Section 4.4 indicate that if a program runs successfully on $h\log(h)$ input cases, then the probability of our being wrong in assuming that $\theta < 1/h$ is less than $1/h$. It is important to emphasize that all of this depends on the continued use of the program over the same operational distribution. If it is run on data which is distributed differently from that on which it was tested, the results are invalid.

Continuing research in black-box testing involves the construction of more sophisticated models of the operational distribution of a program's input data.

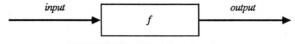

FIGURE 5.1.   Black-box function.

5.3 CONTROL-FLOW COVERAGE MEASURES

The most widely used systematic testing methods involve *test-coverage measures*. A set of program tests is considered *adequate* if all elementary components of a program have been executed at least once on some test of the program. Different measures correspond to different kinds of components.

One of the simplest and most common coverage measures is *branch testing*, in which it is required that each branch through a program be traversed during at least one test execution of the program. Other coverage measures attempt to force the coverage of combinations of branches or statements making up larger parts of the program. Two kinds can be identified: *control-flow* and *data-flow coverage*. The first tries to build bigger program components by examining the flow of control in a program and the second does this by examining the flow of data. Branch testing can be considered to be an elementary form of control-flow coverage.

5.3.1 Statement and Branch Coverage

The easiest kind of coverage measure to implement is *statement coverage*. This involves the use of a tool which can keep track of statement coverage during the execution of a program over a sequence of tests. An obvious shortcoming of statement coverage is its failure to test alternative outcomes of branching statements. Branch testing is the refinement of statement coverage which requires that all branches be tested at least once.

A program branch is any control-flow arc from one program statement to another. In statement-oriented languages there is an implicit branch from one program statement to the next unless the first statement is a *go-to*. In this case there is an explicit branch to some statement out of sequence. There are also implicit branches in compound statements from an outer statement to an inner statement.

The branch structure of a program can be described using a control-flow graph in which the arcs correspond to program branches and the nodes to program statements. Figure 5.2 contains the control-flow graph for the fdl design for *covar* in Figure 2.9.

Branch-testing tools have been used for a long time and have been implemented for a variety of languages.[1,2] Figure 5.3 describes the structure of a simple branch-testing system. It involves several components. The *branch analyzer* analyzes the source program to produce a *branch model* and an *instrumented program*. The instrumented program contains probes which count the number of times program branches are traversed. The *tester* runs the instrumented program against a sequence of test cases, and contains the *branch-traversal table* which is updated by the probes. The *report generator* uses the information in the branch-traversal table, along with the branch model, to construct a complete picture of branch execution.

The details of branch-testing systems will differ for different programming languages, but they all involve the same basic concepts. One of these is the notion of *program location*. This refers to a place in a program at which control can arrive. In a simple language such as Fortran this might be a statement number. More complex ways are needed for identifying loca-

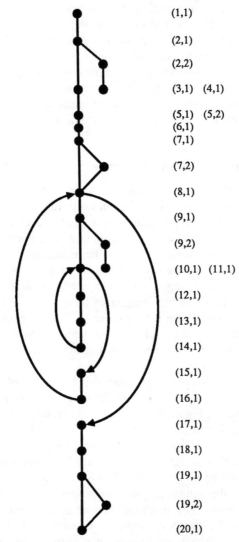

FIGURE 5.2.   Control-flow graph for *covar* with program locations.

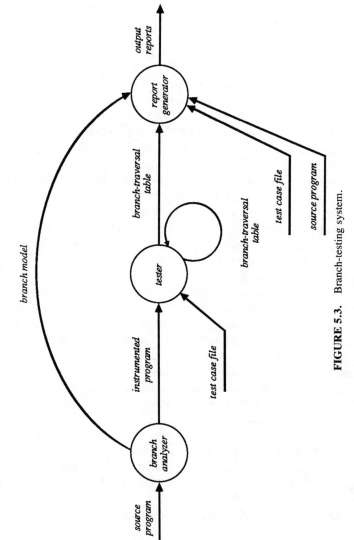

FIGURE 5.3. Branch-testing system.

tions within compound statements in languages such as Pascal. A simple approach is to use pairs of the form:

$$(line\text{-}number, statement\text{-}number).$$

The first element is a source-code-statement line number on which a statement begins. If there is more than one statement that begins on that line, the statement number can be used to distinguish between them. Figure 5.4 contains the program locations for the statement on source line number 19 in the *covar* fdl in Figure 2.9. The flow graph in Figure 5.2 contains the program locations for all of its statements.

Subroutine calls to a *probe monitor* subroutine can be used to insert probes into a program. The calls will have a parameter which tells the probe monitor the program location of the call. The monitor will remember the previous location sent to it and use the location pair (*previouslocation,thislocation*) to update a branch-traversal table. In the simplest case, a probe is inserted at every program location and the branch-traversal table will have an entry for every program branch. A more complex scheme can be used to try to minimize the number of probe insertions and the size of the branch-traversal table. One way is to insert probes only at locations to which control is transferred conditionally. A sophisticated report generator could use the information generated by such probes, together with an appropriate branch model, to reconstruct a complete history of branch traversal.

A branch model for a program can be constructed which consists of a table of triples ($n_1, n_2, branchdescriptor$) where n_1 and n_2 are program locations and *branchdescriptor* contains information about the branch. If the simple-minded approach is being used and probes are inserted at every program location, then the branch model will simply contain information about each branch, such as whether it is the true or false branch from a conditional statement, or a loopexit branch. It may also contain more detailed information, such as the actual predicate associated with a branch, to allow more complicated kinds of reports to be generated.

If an attempt is being made to minimize the required number of probe insertions, then the branch model may also contain for each pair (n_1, n_2) a list of the actual branches which are traversed when the program location pair is encountered during a program execution. The traversal count for these branches will be the same as that which is recorded for the pair (n_1, n_2) in the branch-traversal table. The report generator can use the branch model to recover the complete branch execution information.

$$\text{if } cvf = 1 \text{ then}\quad transformacptovcv(vcv,m)\qquad 19$$
$$\uparrow\qquad\qquad\quad\uparrow$$
$$(19,1)\qquad\qquad (19,2)$$

FIGURE 5.4.   Program locations.

Branch traversers are often constructed to record additional kinds of information. Examples include the minimum and maximum numbers of iterations of the executions of a loop construct, the minimum and maximum values of all variables which are assigned values, and the values of subroutine and function parameters for each subroutine or function invocation. The recording of these additional kinds of information can be done in min-max value tables and parameter call lists, which will also become part of the *tester* program. They will be accessed by the probe monitor subroutine which is invoked by the subroutine call probes in the instrumented source code.

Perhaps the most useful kind of output report which can be generated for branch testing is one which prints the source code, and alongside of it, the branch-testing statistics. Figure 5.5 indicates what such output might look like for part of the fdl for *covar* in Figure 2.9. The output indicates that the implicit branches to the next statement for the first three statements were traversed 521 times. The true branch from the conditional statement was traversed 520 times and the false branch only once. The loop was iterated a total of 52,100 times and the loop exit branch taken only 10 times, indicating that there were 10 executions of the loop construct taken as a whole.

Branch testing can leave many errors undiscovered. Sometimes a fault will be revealed by only some data, but not all data, which causes a branch to be followed. In other cases the fault is associated with a combination of program branches, and a test of that combination of branches is needed to cause the error.

5.3.2 Path Coverage

Various attempts have been made to extend branch testing to larger program components than branches in order to detect faults associated with combinations of program branches. An early suggestion for a more sophisticated form of control-flow coverage was to try to test as many complete program paths as possible. Of course a program containing a loop may have an infinite number of paths. First there is the path which goes around the loop

$$
\begin{array}{ll}
\vdots & \\
k \leftarrow 0; \quad eof \leftarrow \text{false} & 521 \\
& 521 \\
getablockofdata(f, temp, mxblk, m, k, szblk, eof) & 521 \\
\textit{if sf} = 1 \textit{ then getscalingfactorsfromobservations}(temp, sfac) & \text{true: } 520 \\
& \text{false: } 1 \\
\textit{repeat while } k < m & \text{repeat: } 52100 \\
& \text{exit: } 10 \\
\vdots &
\end{array}
$$

FIGURE 5.5.   Branch-testing statistics.

exactly once, then the one which goes around it twice, and so on. But intuitively, once a loop has been tested using a path which iterates it once or twice, it seems as though it should be unnecessary to continue testing other paths which are the same except that they cause more traversals of the loop.[3]

Unfortunately, even if path testing is limited to the testing of all paths which cause only one or two iterations of a loop, there will often still be an enormous number of paths to test. Consider the flow graph in Figure 5.2. It has 79 paths like this. The situation can be much worse. The simple flow graph in Figure 5.6 contains 1852 paths which do not iterate a loop more than twice.

Even when a program is simple enough to have a small number of paths which do not traverse loops more than once or twice, it is often not enough just to test all such paths. There are always faults which are associated with more complex patterns of loop iterations such as "traverse the outer loop three times and the inner loop twice. On the first traversal of the outer loop follow the true-true path through the inner loop conditions on the first traversal of the inner loop, and the false-false path on the second traversal of the inner loop. On the second traversal of the outer loop reverse

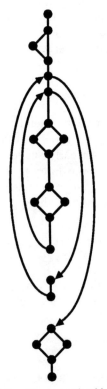

FIGURE 5.6.   Simple graph with many paths.

the traversal pattern on the inner loop and on the last traversal of the outer loop go back to the original traversal pattern for the inner loop." Patterns of loop traversal like this may seem to correspond to various functional cases in the data, but there are so many such patterns that the idea of cataloguing them and using them to specify which paths to test is impractical.

An *infeasible* path is a path through a program which is never traversed for any input data. This is because the logical conditions that would have to be satisfied to cause this path to be followed are contradictory. Such paths are not necessarily caused by program faults; the paths are just coincidental artifacts of the program structure. Consider, for example, the program fragment in Figure 5.7. This Fortran program, described by Hedley and Hennell,[4] is a widely used example in program testing. It reads three integers and decides if they could be the sides of a triangle. It also decides what kind of triangle it is (scalene, isosceles, or equilateral). Consider a path which takes the true branch at statements 9, 10, and 11, and takes the MATCH−1=0 branch at statement 12. The following set of path conditions will be generated for this subpath.

$$J.EQ.K$$

$$K.EQ.L$$

$$L.EQ.J$$

$$2=0$$

The last predicate ($2=0$) occurs when MATCH−1 in statement 12 evaluates to 2. This path is trivially infeasible because it results in an impossible path

```
 1            READ (5,100) J, K, L
 2            WRITE (6,100) J, K, L
 3     100    FORMAT (3I10)
 4            IF (J + K.GT.L .AND. K + L.GT.J .AND. L + J.GT.K) GO TO 1
 5            WRITE (6,101)
 6     101    FORMAT (15H NOT A TRIANGLE)
 7            STOP
 8       1    MATCH = 0
 9            IF (J.EQ.K) MATCH = MATCH + 1
10            IF (K.EQ.L) MATCH = MATCH + 1
11            IF (L.EQ.J) MATCH = MATCH + 1
12            IF (MATCH − 1) 2,3,4
13       2    WRITE (6,102)
14     102    FORMAT (17H SCALENE TRIANGLE)
15            STOP
16       3    WRITE (6,103)
17     103    FORMAT (19H ISOSCELES TRIANGLE)
18            STOP
19       4    WRITE (6,104)
20     104    FORMAT (21H EQUILATERAL TRIANGLE)
21            STOP
22            END
```

FIGURE 5.7. Triangle program.

predicate. In more complex examples, systems of path predicates are infeasible because two or more predicates, which by themselves may be satisfiable, when taken together are contradictory.

If the percentage of paths in a program which are infeasible is very high, and if there were some way of automatically eliminating them, then path testing might become practical. In a study of 6 of the NAG Algol68 library of numerical analysis routines, it was found that an average of only 18 out of the first 1000 shortest paths through the programs were feasible.[5] These statistics are very promising, indicating that not only path testing but other testing and analysis methods which rely on looking at program paths may be able to avoid the path explosion problem. Techniques for doing this are described later in the section on predicate-system solutions and infeasible paths.

It should be noted that even if it were possible to detect and discard infeasible paths, and if the percentage of these were high, allowing the consideration of all paths which iterate loops less than, say, three times, there are still serious problems with path testing. Many errors will not be discovered unless a path is traversed which requires that a loop be iterated a large number of times, and there is still the problem of choosing what data to use for testing a feasible path from amongst all the data which causes that path to be followed.

5.3.3 Control-Flow Coverage and Functional Testing

Control-flow methods can be interpreted as crude attempts to approximate functional testing in the following sense. If all parts of a program are tested, then hopefully, all of the requirements, design, and programming functions embedded in the program will have been tested at least once. This is only partly true. Suppose that branch coverage is used. Then every low-level function which corresponds to a single statement will be tested at least once, as well as the function corresponding to the program as a whole. But there is no guarantee that functions which correspond to parts of the program intermediate in size between a single statement and the whole program will have been tested, since they may correspond to combinations of branches that are left untested. The extension of branch testing to path testing, or to special classes of subpaths (e.g., linear code and jump subpaths[5]), can be thought of as attempts to explicitly identify and test these larger functions. In addition to the problems with path testing previously described, there is also the problem that many functions will not correspond to individual paths or parts of paths. Many paths, even if feasible, will correspond only to parts of functions rather than whole functions. There does not appear to be any generally successful way of identifying functions by analyzing a program's control-flow structure.

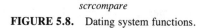

getclientsinfo	*dater*	*halfbliss*
matchscore	*getrequest*	*readdatabase*
getdatesinfo	*getclient*	
bestdate	*getdt*	
	updt	
	blissf	
	scrcompare	

FIGURE 5.8.   Dating system functions.

There are two ways in which the approach to functional testing introduced in the preceding chapters can be used to refine control-flow coverage and ameliorate the problems described. The first is to require the identification and explicit testing of the parts of a program that implement functions which occur in requirements, specifications, and design. Figure 5.8 lists the requirements and design functions for the dating program example, and Figure 5.9, the *covar* functions. The first column in each figure contains the requirements functions, the second, the general design functions, and the third, additional detailed design functions. Functional testing requires that each of these functions be tested. They can be tested separately using a test harness to run just those parts of a program that correspond to a function or they can be tested within the context of the program as a whole, by printing out the values of variables which carry input into the functions at the point where the code corresponding to the functions is entered, and printing out the values of variables which carry data out of the functions where the functions are exited. Note that functions may or may not correspond to sections of code that are specifically identified as subroutines, procedures, or functions in a program. In general, as in the examples given, many design functions will correspond to partial routines or procedures, to subsections of code that are not encapsulated in a programming language construct.

The second way in which functional testing can be used to refine control-flow coverage is in its identification of the data over which input-output functions should be tested.

scfac	*covar*	*symindxf*
meanf	*infile*	*valinf*
crossprf	*indata*	*szblkf*
	update	*initializearrays*
	psumf	*getablockofdata*
	pucpf	*getscalingfactors-*
	meanvcvf	*fromobservations*
	meanacpf	*updatepsum*
	meanf	*updatepucp*
	acpf	*constructmean -*
	vcvf	*fromsum*
		transformucptoacp
		transformacptovcv

FIGURE 5.9.   *covar* program functions.

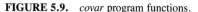

Input-output functions were characterized in Chapter 4 as being those for which there is an input-output oracle. They were also identified as being formed by expression, conditional, and iterative synthesis, and their faults as being those of the synthesizing operations. Test data which was capable of revealing simple faults was described. Since expressions, conditional branches, and iteration statements are very low-level constructs, it may appear that the theory of functional testing can only be used to refine the testing procedures for very low-level input-output functions—those at the statement and branch level. This would still be an improvement over branch and statement testing because it would not only indicate that these constructs should be tested, but would also indicate the data over which they should be tested. But it would still leave the problem of choosing test data for higher-level functions, those corresponding to parts of program paths, and so on, unsolved. Fortunately, functional testing resolves this problem.

The requirement that all functions be examined individually, plus the assumption that all input-output functions can be represented as syntheses of lower-level functions, is all that is needed to force the examination of higher-level functions over fault-revealing test data. Even though a function may correspond to a part of a program which is bigger than an individual statement, it is assumed to have been constructed from other functions using a synthesizing operation at the statement level. If all faults in input-output functions are synthesis faults, then all that is necessary to force the testing of functions over fault-revealing test data is to require, during the examination of each function, that all function statements be tested over fault-revealing test data.

Note that even though statement coverage rules can be used to force the testing of all functions over fault-revealing data, it is still necessary to identify the sections of code corresponding to different embedded functions in a program. Techniques for automating this part of functional testing, which are more promising than the methods involving control flow previously discussed, are covered later in Section 5.5.

It is not always the case that one function is formed by a simple synthesizing operation in a hierarchical fashion from lower-level, correct, or previously tested functions. Programs formed in this way would have a structure like that in the example in Figure 5.10. In practice, programmers construct functions which are synthesized from a collection of functions which are interwoven to work together in a cooperative manner. Functions like this are synthesized using structures and are validated using the structural analysis techniques described in Chapter 6.

5.4 FUNCTIONAL TESTING RULES

The method of functional testing is to identify each of the functions implemented in a program and then to examine its input-output behavior over

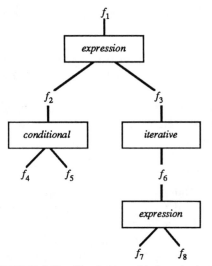

FIGURE 5.10. Simple hierarchical synthesis.

appropriate functional test data. The statements in a program are viewed as structures used to synthesize functions. Program faults are viewed as faults in these synthesizing statements and failures can be discovered using tests which cause the statements to be executed over the appropriate data. The data which is needed for uncovering common classes of faults was described in the theory of functional testing in Chapter 4. The following subsections review the simpler and more practical fault-revealing testing rules for each of the statement-oriented synthesizing operations.

5.4.1 Expressions

The theoretical results for testing expressions (i.e., for detecting faults in functions formed by expression synthesis) were of two kinds. The nonstatistical results described tests guaranteed to find specific classes of faults. The problem with these results was that they were practical only for simple faults or simple expressions. The statistical results proved that a single randomly chosen point would probably reveal any fault in an expression of any complexity. The problem with this result is that if an expression is buried inside a program, and the values of its variables are computed in the program and are not program input variables, it may be difficult to choose input data so that when control reaches the expression it is executed over random data. Random input data for the program can be selected, but by the time the expression is reached, the data may have been operated on in such a way that it can no longer be considered random.

Fortunately, most program expressions and program expression faults are simple. The first functional testing rule for expressions will reveal faults in any expression in which the fault is a single incorrect expression coefficient.

1. Test expressions over data such that individual variables all have nonzero values and the expression evaluates to a nonzero value.

The effectiveness of this rule for revealing single coefficient errors in arbitrary expressions of the form

$$\frac{f_1(x)}{f_2(x)}$$

where f_1 and f_2 are arbitrary polynomials in one or more variables is proved by Theorem 4.4. The theorem requires that both the given and correct expressions be defined over the test data. If the given expression in the program is not defined, presumably the presence of a fault will be detected immediately. It is assumed that it is known when the correct expression is undefined.

More complex faults can be detected if the class of expressions is more restricted. The following rule, whose effectiveness was proved in the corollary to Theorem 4.6, will work for faults in linear expressions in which more than one coefficient is incorrect.

2. Suppose the variables in the expression are $x_1, x_2, .., x_n$. Then select $n+1$ tests $(x_{i,1}, x_{i,2}, \ldots, x_{i,n})$, $1 \le i \le n+1$, which cause the matrix in Figure 5.11 to be nonsingular.

This test will reveal all errors in which one or more coefficients is incorrect. Consider, for example, the expression

$$2x + y - 1.$$

Then the tests in Figure 5.12 will reveal any incorrect coefficient error in the expression since the associated matrix is nonsingular.

The only practical method for testing for complex faults in complex expressions is to use the following statistically effective rule.

3. Test the expression over a randomly chosen input case.

FIGURE 5.11. Linear expressions test matrix.

$$x = 1 \quad y = 2$$
$$x = 2 \quad y = 5$$
$$x = 3 \quad y = 11$$

FIGURE 5.12. Linear tests example.

If the expression is complex, there is a good chance that it is a function in and of itself. If it does not synthesize a more complex function from subfunctions, then it can be isolated and tested individually over a random test case. The effectiveness of rule (3) is proved in Theorems 4.8 through 4.10.

5.4.2 Conditional Branching

The functional testing rules for conditional statements of the form

$$\text{if } b \text{ then } s_1 \text{ else } s_2$$

depend on the structure of the Boolean condition b. In addition, it is necessary to choose tests which cause the functions initiated by the then and else parts of the statement to give different results. In the simplest case the then and else functions correspond exactly to the s_1 and s_2 parts of the statement. In less structured programs, especially if s_1 or s_2 is a *go-to*, the then and else functions may include sections of code in other parts of the program. In general, it may be necessary to require that the test data be such that the program as a whole computes different output for the control flows associated with the then and else conditional choices.

Research on how to force two program components to return different output values has been carried out by Morell and Hamlet[6] and by Zeil,[7] but it is a difficult problem for which there are no simple, practical rules. For the purposes of automated test coverage analysis it will be necessary to compromise and settle on some approximation to the theoretical ideal. The suggested approximation is to assume that the functions selected by b are just s_1 and s_2 by themselves and to require that on each test at least one of the variables assigned values in the s_1 statement be assigned a different value from what it would receive in the s_2 statement.

The first functional testing rule for conditionals can be used to reveal simple arithmetic relation faults and is based on Theorem 4.14.

1. Suppose the Boolean relation b in a conditional is of the form *exp rel* 0 where *rel* is $<$, $\leq$, $>$, $\geq$, $\neq$, or $=$, and *exp* is an arithmetic expression. Suppose that either *exp* is off by an additive constant (i.e., should be $exp+k$ for some $k \neq 0$) or *rel* is the wrong relational operator. Then this fault can be detected using tests which cause *exp* to take on its largest negative value (*maxneg*), zero, and its smallest positive value (*minpos*). In addition, the two alternative functions that can be selected by the conditional must give different values for the data used in the tests.

This rule can be easily augmented to take care of the simple extension to the case where *exp* is a conjunctive expression of the form:

$$exp_1 \; rel_1 \; 0 \text{ and } exp_2 \; rel_2 \; 0 \text{ and} \ldots \text{and } exp_n \; rel_n \; 0$$

or a disjunctive of the form:

$$exp_1 \; rel_1 \; 0 \text{ or } exp_2 \; rel_2 \; 0 \text{ or} \ldots \text{or } exp_n \; rel_n \; 0.$$

The rule, based on Theorems 4.22 and 4.23, becomes:

2. Construct tests so that each term $exp_i \; rel_i \; 0$ in the compound expression is tested over a set of tests satisfying the condition of rule (1) while at the same time, for conjunctive Booleans, all other terms are held to the value true and, for disjunctive Booleans, all other terms are held to false.

These rules can be used for arbitrary expressions. Theorem 4.21 in Chapter 4 describes special rules for selecting test data when *exp* is of the form either *x rel y* or *x rel k* and *x* and *y* are defined over discrete ordered domains. The rules specified actual values for *x, y,* and *k* which would cause *exp* to have the required properties for the application of rules (1) and (2) above. The results in the theorem could also be incorporated into rules which could be used to build a functional test coverage tool for conditionals, but the more general rules are suggested. The special purpose rules can be used as guidelines for the programmer for selecting data which satisfies the general rules.

If it is desired to also consider "wrong variables" faults, then there are two possible rules to be used in conjunction with the other rules. Suppose that the Boolean function is a relation of the form *exp rel* 0 or a conjunctive or disjunctive compound relation containing terms of this type. Let *exp'* be the expression resulting from the substitution of a potential wrong variable in *exp*. Then *exp* can be distinguished from *exp'* using the following rule.

3. Choose tests that satisfy rules (1) or (2) above and, in addition, choose values for the potential wrong variable so that either:

(i) $exp' < 0$ on all three tests or $exp' > 0$ on all three tests; or

(ii) (exp'_1, exp'_2, exp'_3) the values of exp' in the three tests, is a right- or left-shift permutation of (exp_1, exp_2, exp_3) the values of *exp* on the tests. Right- and left-shift permutations are described in Chapter 4.

The difficulty of testing for wrong variables errors in Boolean expressions makes the simpler general purpose rules for wrong variables, which were discussed under alternative algebras in Chapter 4, appear more desirable. These are reviewed later in this chapter.

5.4.3   Iteration

Testing rules for program constructs of the form

$$\text{repeat while/until } b(x) = \text{true}$$
$$s_1$$
$$s_2$$
$$\vdots$$
$$s_n$$
$$\text{endrepeat}$$

will depend both on b and on the statements s_i, $1 \le i \le n$, embedded in the loop. Recall that for while loops the loop termination test is done at the beginning of the loop and for until loops at the end. The required tests for iterative constructs which are specified in Theorem 4.15 impose conditions on the function corresponding to the embedded statements s_i, $1 \le i \le n$, inside the loop. It will be assumed that the variables which are referenced inside the loop are the function's input variables. Those which are assigned values are its output variables. A variable may be both. This convention, together with the theorems for relation testing, can be used to derive the following testing rules for iterative constructs. It is assumed that the Boolean relation in the loop is an arithmetic expression, as in the testing rules for conditional statements, and that possible faults are off by an additive constant or wrong relational operator.

1. Choose a set of tests T so that for each test, one or more of the variables which are assigned values inside the loop get their values changed during each loop iteration. This means that each iteration of the loop during a test will produce a new set of values for the output variables in the loop. Assume that the loop terminates for each test t in T. For each t, each iteration of the loop occurring before termination will produce a new set of values s for the variables in the loop (some or all of the values will change). Let S contain all such sets s for all t in T. An additional property that T must have is that the induced set S will reveal faults in b. For the simple faults previously specified, for Booleans of the form

$$exp \; rel \; 0,$$

there must be elements of S that will cause exp to be *maxneg*, zero, and *minpos* on at least one test. As always, in the testing of Booleans, if no data exists which will cause exp to take on all the required values, it is only necessary to force it to take on all possible values for the tests to be effective.

   If the loop is a while loop, then the set S will include T (the zero iteration values of the loop's variables). If it is an until loop, T is not included, and at least one iteration of the loop must be carried out in generating S. The following simplified rule for while loops is based on the corollary to Theorem 4.15.

2. Choose a test set T which results in *exp* taking on the values *maxneg*, zero, and *maxpos*, and such that the execution of the code in the loop will change the value of at least one output variable for each test in T.

The extension of these rules to the case where the Boolean loop termination expression is a conjunctive or disjunctive form is done in the same way as for conditionals. Each term must have its own subset of tests which are adequate for testing it individually while other terms are forced to evaluate to true (for conjunctives) or false (for disjunctives). The rules can also be extended to wrong loop condition variable faults in the same way but, as in the case for conditionals, it may be desirable to deal with this problem separately.

5.4.4   Wrong-Variable Faults

The retrieval of a value from and the storage of a value into the wrong variable can be thought of as faults in very low-level *retrieve* or *store* functions. These functions can be made to operate incorrectly if the following test rules from Chapter 4 are applied.

1. The value stored into a variable should be different from its current value.
2. The value retrieved from a variable should be different from the values of all other variables.

The rules can be generalized to data structures in the obvious way. The difficulty with these rules is that to test and examine the input-output data for all retrieval and storage operations is extremely tedious. One possible solution to the difficulty is to apply the rules, but only examine their effects indirectly by looking at the input-output behavior of higher-level functions in which the retrieval and store operations are embedded. The problem with this is that the effect of a wrong variable may be masked in a higher-level function.

Perhaps the most potentially useful way to discover wrong-variable faults is to use data-type transformation analysis. If a wrong variable is used, and different variables have different types or flavors, then the fault will cause a type transformation error which can be detected using techniques described in Chapter 6.

5.5   DATA-FLOW COVERAGE MEASURES

Functional testing overcomes two serious problems that occur in branch testing: the failure to test partial program functions and the failure to test constructs over error-revealing test data. The disadvantage of functional testing is that it is not as easily automated as branch testing. However, the functional testing rules described in Chapter 4 which were reviewed in the previous section could be automated. A tool could be built which kept track of the kinds of data over which program statements (i.e., function syntheses) were executed, but it would still be necessary for the programmer to identify the program subpaths and combinations of branches corresponding to functions embedded in the code, to check that they have been tested, and to observe their input-output behavior. If these functions are fully documented in the requirements or the general and detailed design documents, then this is not unmanageable, but it would be convenient if this could be automated also.

In the section on control-flow coverage measures, attempts to extend branch testing to larger program components which are closer to embedded design and programming functions were described. These attempts have not been entirely successful. Another class of test coverage tools, based on data-flow coverage, is more promising. The basic idea is that statements which have a data-flow relationship should be tested together during the same test. Suppose, for example, that statement s_1 computes a value for variable x which is later referenced in statement s_2. Then it is argued that some test should execute s_1 followed by the execution of s_2.

The functional interpretation of data-flow oriented testing is that statements which have a data-flow relationship are probably part of the same embedded function and should be tested together in at least one test. In this interpretation, data-flow coverage testing schemes correspond to primitive attempts to extract functional patterns from code. Two data-flow testing measures will be described.

5.5.1 Definition-Reference Chain Data-Flow Coverage

The first data-flow method is the *dr-chains* (or definition-reference chains) coverage measure. This is a variation on an idea originally suggested by Herman[8] and refined by Ntafos.[9] A definition-reference pair, or a *dr-pair* (d,r), consists of a program component d in which a variable value is defined and a component r in which it is referenced. It is assumed that there is a path from the definitional component to the referencing component along which there is no intervening definition for the variable. The simplest kinds of dr-pairs are pairs of assignment statements where the first statement assigns a value to a variable which is referenced in the second. Others include the parts of a conditional statement. The then and else substatements of a conditional statement are treated as two separate components. Suppose that *cond* is the branch condition in a conditional statement and that variable x is referenced in *cond*. The component *cond* is considered to cause a variable definition since it imposes a constraint on x defined by the condition. If either the then or the else substatements reference x, then the component *cond* and the substatement form a dr-pair. A *1dr-chain* consists of a single dr-pair. A *kdr-chain* consists of a sequence $(p_1, p_2, \ldots, p_k)$ of k dr-pairs $p_i = (d_i, r_i)$, $1 \leq i \leq k$, such that for $1 \leq i < k$, $r_i = d_{i+1}$ (i.e., the referencing component in one pair is the defining component for the next). In the following discussion, components will be assumed to be statements, with the understanding that extra provisions have to be made for conditional statements.

Although it is intuitively clear that kdr-chain coverage will be better than branch coverage, there is little empiricial information on how well it extracts functions from code and on what value of k is most useful.

The preprocessing stage for a dr-chain coverage tool will be more complex than that for a branch coverage tool since it must analyze a program to find its dr-pairs. The actual probes that are inserted into the instrumented code need not be that complex. The preprocessor will be expected to build two tables: a *dr-pair table* and a *reference-definition table*. The dr-pair table will contain an entry for each dr-pair. Each time a dr-pair is encountered during program execution, the probes inserted into the instrumented program will record this in the dr-pair table. The other table will contain an entry for each statement. It will contain a *reference list* of all the variables and parts of data structures which are referenced by this statement. It will also contain a *definition list* of all variables and data structures whose values are defined in this statement. For some languages it may also be necessary to list variables whose values become undefined in a statement without having a new value assigned.

As a program is executed a *current definitions* list is kept. Each element of this list is a pair (*variable, statement*). The first element is a variable or part of a data structure which was assigned a value in the statement designated by the second element of the list. Each time a new statement is reached, the probe in the instrumented program will look to see which of the variables in the current definitions list are in the reference list for that statement. For each of these a dr-pair has been found and the appropriate dr-table entry is updated. The definition list for the encountered statement is examined. If there are new definitions for variables already in the current definitions list, those entries are deleted. New entries are then made in the current definitions list for all new definitions.

This basic design can be optimized in several ways. The dr-pair table need only be a bit map, for example, if all that is required is to record whether a dr-pair has been encountered, and not to count how many times. A complete system must be able to merge coverage statistics from different test runs, as in the case for a branch coverage tool. The identity of statements can be done in the same way as for branch coverage using a source location pair (*line-number, statement-number*).

The procedure described for 1dr-coverage testing can be extended to 2dr coverage in the following way. In addition to a dr-pairs table, the coverage system will also maintain a 2dr table, containing an entry for each possible 2dr-chain in the program. Each element of the current definitions list will include not only a variable and a statement identifier, but also a dr-pair list. Suppose that (v,s,drp) is a current definitions list entry where v is a variable, s a statement identifier, and drp a dr-pair list. This entry will be created for a variable v which is defined in statement s at the time s is encountered. When it is created, the current definitions list is searched and dr-pairs are created for all definitions that are referenced in s. Those dr-pairs are put in the dr-pair list drp for the entry.

Whenever a new dr-pair is encountered it will be because there is a reference in the statement currently being executed to a variable whose definition occurs in the current definitions list. If the current definitions list element for that definition contains a nonempty dr-pairs list, then one or more 2dr-chains has been found. The first pair in any of these chains is any pair in this nonempty dr-pairs list and the second pair is the new dr-pair. All possible such 2dr-chains are constructed and the 2dr table updated.

As in the case of 1dr coverage, each time a new entry is made in the current definitions list, old entries may end up being deleted.

5.5.2 Data-Context Data-Flow Coverage

The dr-chain method treats each data reference in a program individually. Suppose that a statement s contains references to two variables x and y and that there are two dr-pairs for the x reference and two for the y reference. Then there are as many as four different ways in which the definitions in the dr-pairs can provide the data for the x and the y references in the program. Since dr-chain coverage does not require the consideration of the combined set of references appearing in a statement, it may not force the testing of all four possibilities.

Figure 5.13 contains a simple example of this situation. There are four dr-pairs (1,5), (2,5), (3,5), and (4,5). It is possible to test all four with only two tests. Suppose the tests cause the traversal of the program paths (1,3,5) and (2,4,5). Then statement 5 will not have been tested with the combination of data values provided by the combinations of assignments:

$$x \leftarrow a \quad \text{and} \quad y \leftarrow d$$
$$\text{or} \quad x \leftarrow b \quad \text{and} \quad y \leftarrow c$$

Each of the four possible ways in which values can be defined for x and y in the example in Figure 5.13 is a *data context* for statement 5. Data-context flow coverage requires the testing of each of these data contexts.

In general, suppose that s is a program statement and that $(d_1,d_2,\ldots,$ $d_n)$ are assignment statements which provide a complete set of definitions for (i.e., assign values to) each of the variables referenced in s. Assume that the definitions d_i, $1 \leq i \leq n$, all lie on the same path p from the beginning

$$
\begin{array}{lll}
\text{if } cond_1 & \text{then } x \leftarrow a & 1 \\
 & \text{else } x \leftarrow b & 2 \\
\text{if } cond_2 & \text{then } y \leftarrow c & 3 \\
 & \text{else } y \leftarrow d & 4 \\
z \leftarrow x + y & & 5
\end{array}
$$

FIGURE 5.13.   Combinations of data references.

of the program to s, and that each d_i assigns a value to at least one variable in s which receives no other definition along the part of p which goes from d_i to s. Then $(d_1, d_2, \dots, d_n)$ is a *data context* for s. Data-context data-flow coverage, or *dc-coverage*, requires that each of the data contexts in a program be tested on at least one test. Data-context data-flow coverage is derived from the work of Laski and Korel[10] and is related to the work of Rapps and Weyuker.[11]

Data-context data-flow coverage requires the use of a tool which can be used to keep track of which data contexts have been tested over a sequence of tests. A tool can be built which is similar to that for dr-chain testing. A preprocessor will build a table of data contexts and tables listing data definitions and references for statements (including the condition branches for conditional statements). It will also insert probes that will maintain a current definitions list as the program is executed. When a new statement is reached, its references are examined and the current data context constructed from the current definitions list. This is used to update the count in the data contexts table which is used for keeping track of which data contexts have been tested.

Data-context testing is like 1dr-chain coverage in the sense that it only examines data-reference chains of length one. It is possible to consider the extension of simple data-context testing, or *1dc-chain* testing to *2dc-chain* testing, in the same way that 2dr-chain testing is an extension of 1dr-chain testing.

One of the difficulties that occurs in control-flow testing when attempts are made to require the testing of paths is that of infeasibility. This can also occur in data-flow testing. Recall that a path is infeasible if there is no test data which will cause it to be executed. Any requirement that program structures which are larger than single statements be tested may involve the infeasibility problem, and this includes even 1dr-chain or 1dc-chain testing. Although there is a possible flow of data from one statement s_1 to another statement s_2, the conditions associated with this flow may be contradictory and there may be no test data which will cause it to be followed. The ubiquitous nature of the infeasible path (or subpath) problem indicates the importance of finding some method for dealing with it. The most important technique which has been suggested is *symbolic evaluation*. Symbolic evaluation is useful not only for infeasible path analysis, but also for symbolic testing and test data generation.

```
      DOUBLE PRECISION FUNCTION SIN(X,E)      1
  C   THIS COMPUTES SIN(X) TO ACCURACY E      2
      DOUBLE PRECISION E, TERM, SUM            3
      REAL X                                   4
      TERM = X                                 5
      SUM = X                                  6
      DO 20 I = 3,100,2                        7
         TERM = TERM * X ** 2 / (I * (I − 1))  8
         SUM = SUM + ((−1) ** (I / 2)) * TERM  9
         IF (DABS(TERM) .LT.E) GO TO 30       10
  20  CONTINUE                                11
  30  SIN = SUM                               12
      RETURN                                  13
      END                                     14
```

FIGURE 5.14.   Fortran SIN function.

5.6   SYMBOLIC EVALUATION

5.6.1   Basic Concepts

Symbolic evaluation is a technique in which a program is executed over symbols rather than actual values. When an expression is symbolically evaluated, the symbolic values of each of the variables in the expression are substituted into the expression. If the expression occurs on the right-hand side of an assignment, the resulting symbolic value becomes the new symbolic value of the variable on the left of the assignment.

Figure 5.14 contains the code for a simple Fortran program for computing the sine of a number. Suppose that the symbolic value "X" is assigned to the input parameter X and the symbolic value "E" to the input parameter E. If the paths which cause the loop in the program to be iterated one time and two times are symbolically executed, then the function will return the values in Figure 5.15.

Symbolic evaluation can be used to analyze the conditional branching predicates of a program as well as its output computations. Suppose that the one- and two-loop iteration paths whose symbolic outputs appear in Figure 5.15 are executed and that each time the branch predicate in statement 10 is encountered it is symbolically evaluated and printed out. Then the systems of predicates in Figure 5.16 will be generated. The symbolic output values for SIN have also been included.

In order to symbolically execute a program it is necessary to assign symbolic values to its input values and to choose a path through the program

$$SIN = X − X ** 3 / 6$$
$$(a)$$

$$SIN = X − X ** 3 / 6 + X ** 5 / 120$$
$$(b)$$

FIGURE 5.15.   Symbolic output for SIN. (a) Output for one-iteration path.
(b) Output for two-iteration path.

to be evaluated. The choice of a path by the user is usually necessary since symbolic predicates will not, in general, evaluate to true or false, and the symbolic evaluator will not be able to determine which branch to follow from a conditional branching statement.

It is possible to symbolically evaluate a program over mixtures of actual and symbolic data. An expression simplifier can be used which, in addition to simplification of symbolic expressions, can be used to completely evaluate expressions and subexpressions which consist only of actual data. In some examples, symbolic output is more revealing if actual values are used for some variables, such as array indices. It is also sometimes more desirable to examine the trace of intermediate symbolic values assigned to selected variables rather than the final output values. The use of mixed actual and symbolic values in symbolic value traces is illustrated by symbolically executing the Fortran program in Figure 5.17.[12] The program, called PDIV, was derived from a program in a well-known scientific subroutine package. It can be used to carry out polynomial division. It has two input vectors X and Y which contain the coefficients of the polynomials to be divided. The polynomial X is to be divided by the polynomial Y by subtracting successive multiples of Y from X. The input parameters IDIMX and IDIMY contain the dimensions of X and Y, and it is assumed that IDIMX $\geq$ IDIMY > 0. The result of the division is returned in the vector W and the remainder in X.

Suppose that PDIV is executed over the two test cases containing the mixed actual and symbolic data in Figure 5.18. Then the resulting symbolic output traces will be generated for the arrays W and X. Note that it is not necessary for the user to select the paths to be executed in this example since the selection of actual values for input variables IDIMX and IDIMY completely determines the number of times the loops will be iterated. A system which allows mixtures of actual and symbolic values can attempt to choose paths automatically when expressions evaluate to nonsymbolic values.

Symbolic evaluation can be used for symbolic testing, test data generation, infeasible path detection, and proofs of correctness. When symbolic

DABS(X ** 3 / 6).LT.E
$\downarrow$
SUM = X − X ** 3 / 6
(*a*)

DABS(X ** 3 / 6).GE.E
and DABS(X ** 5 / 120).LT.E
$\downarrow$
SUM = X − X ** 3 / 6 + X ** 5 / 120
(*b*)

FIGURE 5.16. Symbolic predicates for SIN. (*a*) Predicate and output for one-iteration path. (*b*) Predicates and output for two-iteration path.

```
SUBROUTINE PDIV(IDIMX,X,IDIMY,Y,W)
DIMENSION X(IDIMX),Y(IDIMY),W(IDIMX − IDIMY + 1)
IDIMW = IDIMX − IDIMY + 1
IDIMX = IDIMY − 1
DO 10 I = IDIMW,1,−1
    II = I + IDIMX
    W(I) = X(II) / Y(IDIMY)
    DO 20 K = 1,IDIMY,1
        J = K − 1 + I
        X(J) = X(J) − W(I) * Y(K)
20      CONTINUE
10  CONTINUE
    RETURN
    END
```

FIGURE 5.17.   Polynomial division routine.

evaluation is used for symbolic testing, it is used to generate symbolic output values that are compared with program requirements and specifications. This implies the need for a symbolic input-output oracle. In the case of scientific programs this can take the form of mathematical formulae which can be compared directly with the symbolic output. This is possible for the SIN example in Figures 5.14 and 5.15.

The theory in Chapter 4 was developed for input-output oracles which examined actual output data and is not relevant for symbolic testing. No theory of symbolic testing has been developed with the exception of attempts to characterize the conditions under which the correct symbolic output from a subset of a program's paths implies the correctness of the symbolic output from all paths.[13] This question has been only partially answered and only for a very simple set of programs.

The symbolic systems of predicates for a program path can be used to describe the input data that will cause that path to be followed. The predicates in Figure 5.16 describe the conditions that must be satisfied by the

```
Input:   IDIMX = 1   IDIMY = 1
         X(1) = X(1)   Y(1) = Y(1)
Trace:   W(1) = X(1) / Y(1)
         X(1) = X(1) − W(1) * Y(1)


Input:   IDIMX = 3   IDIMY = 2
         X(1) = X(1)   Y(1) = Y(1)
         X(2) = X(2)   Y(2) = Y(2)
         X(3) = X(3)
Trace:   W(2) = X(3) / Y(2)
         X(2) = X(2) − W(2) * Y(1)
         X(3) = X(3) − W(2) * Y(2)
         W(1) = X(2) / Y(2)
         X(1) = X(1) − W(1) * Y(1)
         X(2) = X(2) − W(1) * Y(2)
```

FIGURE 5.18.   Symbolic traces for PDIV.

input data X and E in order for the one-iteration and two-iteration paths through the program to be executed. If the symbolic system of predicates for a path does not have a solution, then the path is infeasible. Test data generation and infeasible paths are discussed later in the chapter.

5.6.2 Symbolic Evaluation of Nonalgebraic Programs

The symbolic evaluation examples in the preceding section were very simple. When a program contains only arithmetic operations, it is relatively easy to construct concise, readable symbolic values using algebraic expressions. If the operations are not as concise, as in the case of data processing programs, more complicated techniques are needed. Two broad classes of problems that have to be dealt with are data structures and nonfunctional operations.

Two kinds of data structures and their special symbolic evaluation problems will be considered: arrays and records. The problem with arrays is that if a variable which is being used to index the array has a symbolic value, then it will not be known which array element is being referenced. Suppose, for example, that a program contains an assignment to an array element $X(I)$ where I has a symbolic value, and then contains a reference to $X(2)$ where 2 is in the range of I. It will not be clear whether the value of $X(2)$ is the value assigned to $X(I)$ or some other array element. The program fragment in Figure 5.19, taken from Howden,[14] illustrates the problem. Assume that the READ statement assigns the symbolic value "I" to the variable I. Then, in statement 7, is the value of $X(2)$ zero or ten?

Several solutions have been suggested to the ambiguous array reference problem.[15,16,17] One is to split the path that is being symbolically executed into subpaths, one for each possible disambiguation. In the example in Figure 5.19, this would correspond to splitting the path through the fragment at statement 7, one subpath branching off with $X(2)=0$ and the other with $X(2)=10$. Another possibility is to record the value of Y to be the disjunctive symbolic expression (10 or 0). A third possibility is to denote the value as being ambiguous, and to save the subpaths which lead up to the ambiguous reference and which possibly assign values to the referenced array element. Whenever a request for printing the ambiguous value is made, a message in-

```
              DIMENSION X(10)   1
          5   FORMAT I,I2       2
              DO 10 I = 1,10     3
         10   X(I) = 0          4
              READ 5.I          5
              X(I) = 10         6
              Y = X(2)          7
```

FIGURE 5.19.   Program fragment with ambiguous array reference.

dicating that it is ambiguous is printed along with the program subpaths that could define its value. A fourth possibility would be to require, as in the example in Figures 5.17 and 5.18, that all variables which are used as data structure indices have actual, as opposed to symbolic, values. One way of implementing this is to have an interactive system that queries the user whenever it is necessary to disambiguate a value. Symbolic evaluation can produce complex expressions very quickly and it is for this reason that the simplest approach, that of requiring actual values for indices, is suggested.

The difficulties that are encountered with records have to do with the ability of the user to assign a value to part of a record or to assign a value to a whole record and then reference only part of it. In programming languages such as COBOL or PL/I, this is not a problem when only actual values are involved since records are treated as byte strings and the value of a composite record is simply the concatenation of its parts. The value of a part of a record is the value of the sequence of bytes corresponding to that part. However, symbolic values are indivisible objects that stand for the whole symbolic value of a record and cannot be divided up into byte substrings corresponding to the parts or fields of a record. Similarly, the symbolic value of a record whose component parts have individually been assigned symbolic values is not obvious. The approach to this problem which is described below was suggested in Ariza et al.[18] It involves the use of *explicit* and *implicit* symbolic values. It will be explained using the types of record data structures that are found in COBOL and PL/I.

Consider the COBOL data structure in Figure 5.20. Suppose that data item A is assigned the symbolic value *a*. Then *a* is the explicit symbolic value of A. This explicit assignment to A implies that B, C, D, and E now have new values also. Qualification is used to represent these values. Figure 5.21 describes the implied symbolic values for each of the subordinate data items in A.

Suppose that the values *b* and *c* are assigned to B and C in Figure 5.20. Then these are the explicit values of B and C. It implies that A has a new value, which can be represented as the concatenation of the values of B and C. In this case the value of A would be:

$$concat(b,c).$$

In order to avoid ambiguous implicit symbolic values, it is necessary that whenever a data item is assigned a value the implied effects of that as-

```
01    A
05    B      PIC X(25)
05    C
      10   D      PIC X(12)
      10   E      PIC S99V99
```

FIGURE 5.20.   Sample COBOL record.

item	symbolic value
B	B-OF-A(a)
C	C-OF-A(a)
D	D-OF-C-OF-A(a)
E	E-OF-C-OF-A(a)

FIGURE 5.21. Implied symbolic values of subordinate data items.

signment be carried out. It is also necessary to accommodate all synonymous and overlapping data structures such as those resulting from REDEFINES and RENAMES in COBOL and COMMON and EQUIVALENCE in FORTRAN. Procedures have been described that can be used to do this in COBOL.[18]

In the case where it is possible to assign values to vectors or tables as a whole as well as to individual vector or table elements, the explicit and implicit values approach can be used in the same way as it is used for records. The implied value of a table is the concatenation of the values of its elements. The implied value of a table element is the appropriately qualified part of the explicit value of the table as a whole.

It is also necessary in nonarithmetic programs to find some way to represent nonfunctional operations. A functional operation is one for which there is a simple functional notation for describing the effect of its use. The familiar arithmetic operations, in prefix format, have the functional form:

$$+(x,y) \quad -(x,y), \quad *(x,y), \quad \text{and} \quad \div(x,y).$$

Examples of nonfunctional operations or statements include the INSPECT, STRING, and UNSTRING operations in COBOL. These are more like subroutines than functions and they alter the values of more than one variable. The number of variables involved in the statement is not fixed and the statement can perform different functions, depending on the way in which the statement is used. Figure 5.22 contains an example of a typical STRING statement. It is possible to construct a functional notation to describe the effects of the statement but it would be awkward and its usefulness questionable. One approach to the problem uses a *symbolic values dictionary*. In this approach a dummy symbolic value of the form *dataname.dictionaryindex* is created for each data item whose value is affected by the statement. An entry is then made at position *dictionaryindex* in the symbolic values dictionary for the statement. It consists of the symbolically evaluated form of the state-

```
STRING   X DELIMITED SIZE
         Y DELIMITED "DD"
         INTO W
         POINTER P
         ON OVERFLOW PERFORM STRINGERROR
```
FIGURE 5.22. Typical STRING statement.

```
X  = A
Y  = B
W  = C
P  = D
```

```
STRING   A   DELIMITED SIZE
         B   DELIMITED "DD"
         INTO (W,C)
         POINTER D
         ON OVERFLOW PERFORM STRINGERROR
```

FIGURE 5.23.   Symbolically evaluated STRING statement.

ment. This is constructed as follows. If a data item in the statement is used purely for input and its value is not changed by the statement, then its symbolic value is substituted into the statement. If the value of the data item is changed, then a pair of the form (*dataitemname, dataitemvalue*) is substituted where *dataitemname* is the name of the data item and *dataitemvalue* is its original symbolic value. Figure 5.23 contains, for the indicated initial symbolic values of the statement's data items, the symbolically evaluated form of the STRING statement in Figure 5.22. If this evaluated statement is entered into the symbolic values dictionary with index n, then W and P will be assigned the symbolic values W.n and P.n.

5.6.3   Symbolic Evaluation of Designs

The program design language (pdl) for a design can be symbolically evaluated in the same way as a program. The more functional the pdl is, the more readable the symbolic output. Consider the functional design language (fdl) representation for the *dater* function in the dating system design, reproduced in Figure 5.24. Figure 5.25 contains the functional symbolic output

```
function dater(daterequest)                              1
    clientid ← id(daterequest)                           2
    clmessage ← getdt(clientid)                          3
    if nocl(clmessage) ≠ nil                             4
        then return "error: no such client"             5
    clientinfo ← info(clmessage)                         6
    bscore ← 0                                            7
    initializedtfile                                      8
    repeat while not(enddtfile)                          9
        dateinfo ← getnexdt                             10
        score ← blissf(clientinfo,dateinfo)            11
        if score > bscore                              12
            then bscore ← score                        13
                bdate ← dateinfo                       14
    endrepeat                                           15
    return(bdate)                                       16
endfunction                                             17
```

FIGURE 5.24.   Fdl for dating system *dater* function.

$nocl(getdt(id(daterequest))) \neq nil$
$\downarrow$
"error: no such client"

(a)   *error message output*

$nocl(getdt(id(daterequest))) = nil$
$not(enddtfile) = false$
$\downarrow$
?bdate?

(b)   *zero-loop iteration output*

$nocl(getdt(id(daterequest))) = nil$
$not(enddtfile) = true$
$blissf(info(getdt(id(daterequest))),getnextdt) > 0$
$not(enddtfile(enddtfile)) = false$
$\downarrow$
getnexdt

(e)   *one-loop iteration output*

FIGURE 5.25.   Symbolic output for *dater* fdl.

for three paths through the design. Both the predicate systems and any data returned by the function are included. The first output is for the error message path. The second and third are for paths that cause zero and one iterations of the loop. The convention is used in the symbolic output that if a function has no arguments, it accesses a sequential type data structure so that the data it returns can be denoted using a nested sequence of function applications. The symbolic input value of an input variable is the name of the input variable. The notation *?variablename?* is used to denote the undefined value of a variable. The symbolic output reveals a possible undefined value error in the fdl.

5.6.4   Symbolic Evaluation Systems

The structure and capabilities of a symbolic evaluation system will vary according to the programming language to be symbolically evaluated, the purposes of the system, and the desired style of user action. Two of the more important design topics are *path traversal* and *statement evaluation*.

A single-path system can execute only one path at a time. A multipath system is capable of saving the symbolic evaluation context when it comes to an *n*-way branch in a path, following the path that goes down one branch and then returning to follow the paths that go down other branches. There are several alternative ways for the user to specify a path or paths. In a fully interactive system, the user is queried whenever a branch is reached. The user is expected to specify which branch(es) to follow. In a batch system, the user specifies, in a path description language, which path(s) to follow and this specification is supplied to the system before symbolic evaluation begins. In an automated system, all paths are followed which are feasible and which do not go around loops more than some small number of times. In practice there may be too many of these and a mixture of automated and batch or automated and interactive approaches will be needed.

The statement evaluation component of a system will carry out the symbolic evaluation of individual statements, and will depend on the use of a symbolic memory for keeping track of symbolic values. The statement evaluator may also have to deal with mixed actual and symbolic values, and expression simplification. If the solution to the data structure indexing problem is to be solved by requiring that all indexing expressions evaluate to actual values, then the system will have to include an expression evaluator that can perform simplification.

The basic features of the path traverser and statement evaluation modules, as well as other modules and their module interaction, will be described for a general purpose symbolic evaluator that can be used to symbolically evaluate either single or multiple paths through a program and can be operated in interactive, batch, or automatic mode. Its modular structure is outlined in Figure 5.26.

The *preprocessor* module uses the *source code* module to access the source code program. It translates the source code into a convenient format and stores it in the *object code* module. It also builds a *symbolic memory* which can be used to store and retrieve symbolic values and a *symbolic file* system which can be used to store and retrieve symbolic files and records.

The *path traverser* is the principal driver module for the system. It keeps track of the traversal of paths through a program, including the saving

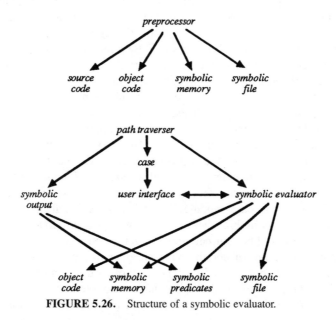

FIGURE 5.26.   Structure of a symbolic evaluator.

and restoring of symbolic evaluation contexts necessary when a path splits at a conditional branch and both paths are to be followed. The path traverser starts at the beginning of the program and for each statement it asks the *case module* if there are any symbolic evaluation commands associated with the statement. If there is more than one branch from the statement, the case module must tell it which branch(es) to follow. If there is more than one branch, and the case module tells it to follow more than one, the path traverser saves the symbolic evaluation context and starts down the path associated with the first of these. When the end of the path is reached, it will restore the symbolic evaluation context and start down the path which follows the next branch. For each statement the path traverser will cause the symbolic evaluation of the statement by calling the *symbolic evaluation* module. The symbolic evaluation module evaluates statements. This may result in new symbolic values for variables being stored in the symbolic memory. If the statement involves a conditional branch, the symbolic evaluation of the branch condition will result in a symbolic predicate. The system of symbolic predicates for the current path is stored in the *symbolic predicates* module. After all paths have been followed the path traverser will return to the subsystem level at which time the user may request the generation of various output reports showing symbolic values of variables and predicates.

The case module can take on different forms, depending on whether interactive or batch mode is desired. A *symbolic evaluation command language* will consist of commands for carrying out various actions, such as declaring the branches to be followed for a conditional branching statement, assigning symbolic values to variables, recording the current symbolic values in the symbolic output, telling the path traverser to terminate a path, or telling the path traverser to terminate the symbolic evaluation. If an interactive case module is used, it will ask the user what to do when a new statement is reached, and he can respond by typing the appropriate symbolic evaluation command(s). In the batch mode the user prepares a set of commands beforehand called a *case*. Each command in the case is stored along with a statement position. Whenever a new statement position is given to the case program, it looks through the current case to find all commands associated with the statement position and causes their execution.

An automatic case program could also be written which, for example, would cause the traversal of all paths up to repeated execution of statements. It would maintain a statement count and whenever a statement was executed for the second time return a terminate path message to the path traverser.

Whenever the case module finds a command that affects path traversal, such as selecting branches to be followed or a skip to a new statement, this information will be returned to the path traverser. If a command is found requesting the output of certain symbolic data, the case module interfaces with the symbolic output module. The symbolic output module accesses the symbolic memory and symbolic predicates modules to obtain the desired symbolic information. At the termination of a symbolic evaluation session, the user, at the subsystem level, can request the saving or printing of the symbolic output which has been generated.

An automatic path traversal case module that is capable of detecting infeasible paths will interact with the symbolic predicates module. Each time a new conditional branching statement is reached, the case module will retrieve the symbolic predicates for the current path and see if the addition of any of the new branch predicates would make it infeasible. If so, the branches causing the infeasibility will not be followed.

The *user interface* interacts with both the case module and the symbolic evaluator. Interactive case modules will request symbolic evaluation commands via the user interface. Batch case modules will not interact with the user interface. The *symbolic evaluator* will interact with the user when it encounters an error, for example, if the user had specified that the *loopexit* branch should be taken from a nonloop control statement. The user is asked for a correct command by the symbolic evaluator via the user interface. This approach is suggested for both iterative and batch case modules.

The symbolic evaluator contains a *symbolic evaluation procedure* for each of the different kinds of statements in the programming language being symbolically evaluated. It calls on the *symbolic memory* module to store and retrieve symbolic values of variables and data structures, and on the *symbolic file* module to store and retrieve symbolic values of records. It records the symbolically evaluated branch predicates it encounters using the *symbolic predicates* module. The *object code* module is used to retrieve the actual object code for a program statement to be symbolically evaluated. Communication between the path traverser and the symbolic evaluator is carried out in terms of statement locations. When the actual statement is needed, the object code module is called upon.

The symbolic evaluator will also include any expression simplification procedures used in constructing symbolic values.

5.7 INFEASIBLE PATHS AND AUTOMATED TEST DATA SELECTION

Symbolic evaluation can be combined with rules for determining if a system of relations has a solution to determine if a program path or subpath is feasible. Suppose, for example, that a program path is symbolically evaluated and its symbolic system of predicates has the form described in Figure 5.27. Then Theorem 4.25 shows how the system can be reduced to a single rela-

$$x \ rel_1 \ y$$
$$x \ rel_2 \ y$$
$$\vdots$$
$$x \ rel_n \ y$$

FIGURE 5.27. Simple path predicate system.

tion or to false. If it reduces to false, the path is infeasible and need not be tested.

Figure 5.28 contains another simple system of predicates. In this case, the rules and the table in Theorem 4.28 can be used to determine feasibility. Systems like those in Figures 5.27 and 5.28 are very simple but have widespread applicability. One reason is that many predicate systems are simple. Another is that in order for a path to be infeasible, it is only necessary that a subset of its system of predicates be infeasible, so that the rules can be applied to the simple subsets of a more complex system of predicates. Of course this will not detect all infeasible paths, but empirical evidence indicates that it is just such simple subsystems that make many paths infeasible. In a study of 88 numerical analysis routines, for example, Hedley and Hennell[4] found that 53 percent of the infeasible paths were due to simple predicates involving loop bounds. Consider the simple Fortran example in Figure 5.29(a). The path which enters the outer loop, traverses the inner loop twice, and then exits the outer loop, will have the branch predicate system in Figure 5.29(b). The predicate $N=1$ is generated because the outer loop is traversed only once, indicating that N must be 1. However, the inner loop was traversed twice, indicating that N must be 2. This simple, infeasible system of predicates has the form described in Figure 5.28, and the rules of Theorem 4.28 can be used to determine its infeasibility.

The applicability of even very simple rules indicates that a feasibility analysis component of a testing or analysis tool would be of great practical importance. Feasibility analysis is particularly important for some of the functional analysis techniques described in the following chapter.

It has been suggested that symbolic evaluation be used not only for path feasibility analysis, but for automating test data generation. This is a potentially more difficult problem. For simple examples of systems such as those in Figures 5.27 and 5.28, it would be easy to generate test data automatically from the predicate system. But unlike feasible path detection, test data generation requires the consideration of the complete set of symbolic predicates for a path; it is not possible to consider simple subsets, unless they are totally independent. A single complex predicate may make test data generation impossible.

One of the early symbolic evaluation systems, SELECT,[15] contained a facility for solving linear systems of inequalities. Other systems had various other predicate analysis capabilities[17] but none, a general facility for solving

$$x\ rel_1\ k_1$$
$$x\ rel_2\ k_2$$
$$\vdots$$
$$x\ rel_n\ k_n$$

FIGURE 5.28.   Single variable path predicate system.

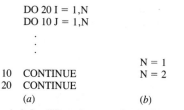

FIGURE 5.29.   Simple infeasible paths example. (*a*) Program. (*b*) Predicates.

predicate systems. Further empirical studies may reveal that most predicate systems fall into a small number of special classes for which special purpose test data generation rules can be designed. A simple test data generation capability could have important uses. Suppose, for example, it was found that some program component had not been executed on any of the tests in a set. Then a path analysis tool with infeasible-path-detection capabilities could construct a path through the program which executed that construct. An automated test generator could then generate test data that would cause it to be executed. Early attempts to provide similar but less ambitious test data generation assistance were incorporated in RXVP[19] and in the much simpler testing tool described by Krause, Smith, and Goodwin.[20]

5.8   AUTOMATED TEST ORACLES

Functional testing depends on the availability of a test oracle which can be used to determine the correctness of the output for a particular test input. Several different kinds of tools have been developed which can be used to automate the management of output verification in functional testing. Two kinds will be discussed: *test harnesses* and *dynamic assertions*.

5.8.1   Test Harnesses

Test harnesses can be used to automatically apply a selected set of test cases to a program and to verify the correctness of the resulting test output. They require that the user construct a set of *test cases*. Each case will provide values for input variables and describe the expected values of output variables.

Sophisticated test harnesses will allow a user to start up a system or program at some intermediate point of execution and to test values at intermediate points. This will require the definition of a location in a program. The approach described earlier in Section 5.3.1 for branch testing can be used. Each test case will describe initial variable values, a starting location, a termination location, and expected terminal variable values.

It may be neither necessary nor possible to specify actual output values; only properties of and relationships between the expected values of variables may be known. This suggests the use of a test case language which allows the user to make assertions about variable values and relations. Typical assertions describe variable ranges and arithmetic relationships between variables.

5.8.2 Dynamic Assertions

Suppose that *loc* is some location in a program and that *assert* is an assertion about program variable values that is always correct at that location, regardless of which input data the program is run on. Then *assert* is an *invariant assertion*. Invariant assertions are similar to the output assertions used in test harnesses. They describe properties of and relationships between variable values at some program location. The difference is that the output assertions in a test case are only required to hold for the specific input described in that test case.

The input independence property of invariant assertions makes it possible to insert them directly into, and for them to become part of, a program. In the dynamic assertion approach to automating test oracles, the user constructs dynamic assertions and inserts them in critical places in the program. The assertions must either be directly executable code or be translatable by an assertion preprocessor into code. Dynamic assertion preprocessors are based on assertion languages which allow users to describe a fixed set of properties of, and relationships between, data.[21] The assertions are called dynamic because they are executed either directly or after translation by a preprocessor.

The error-detection effectiveness of dynamic assertions has been reported to be good[22] although ultimately, of course, their effectiveness depends primarily on the choice of input data over which the program is tested. There are several reasons, however, why they are more than just a convenience for checking the intermediate values of variables, which may explain their effectiveness. The first is their emphasis on the examination of intermediate rather than final variable values. This is consistent with the philosophy in functional testing that intermediate variable values corresponding to intermediate functional input and output must be examined in order to test faults in functions that correspond to parts of programs and program subpaths. Another possible reason for the effectiveness of dynamic assertions is their invariance. Their use forces the programmer to formulate descriptions of the data-independent states of a program or system at critical points in its execution. Looking at a system in terms of its states rather than its state transformation functions provides an alternative, orthogonal point of view.

The use of state assertions in programs was originally associated with proofs of correctness. Proofs of correctness require that the user construct complete formal state descriptions for a program or system, such as the formal fdl states for the *covar* example in Figure 3.10. It is necessary to insert sufficient assertions so that every loop is cut by (i.e., has in its control flow) at least one assertion. In addition, assertions must be detailed enough to allow the proof that the subpaths which link assertions together transform the input assertions for the program into the desired output assertion. The input and output assertions are often referred to as the program's specification. The cost and difficulties of proofs led to the dynamic assertion approach, which can be interpreted as a crude approximation to proofs of correctness.

There are few guidelines for the construction and placement of dynamic assertions. If they are thought of as weak substitutes for assertion-based proving, then they should be as close to complete formal state descriptions as is reasonable and should be inserted so that every possible loop is cut at least once. If they are thought of as automated test oracles for functional testing, then they should be positioned at the places where embedded program functions begin and end. Intuitively, these will correspond to places where the programmer can make general remarks about what is happening in a program, and can serve as comments.

5.9 SUMMARY

The most widely used testing tools are statement and branch coverage monitors. Simple test coverage measures such as branch and statement coverage can be interpreted as crude attempts to force the testing of the functions implemented in a program. From the point of view of functional testing, they have several serious drawbacks. It is often not enough, for example, to test just a statement or branch over some data; it must be tested over fault-revealing test data. In addition, statement-level coverage does not force the testing of functions that correspond to combinations of branches and statements that are intermediate in size between individual statements and the program as a whole. Functional testing rectifies these deficiencies by requiring that programmers independently test sections of code corresponding to intermediate functions, and by requiring that the basic constructs used to synthesize functions, expressions, and conditional and iterative statements be tested over fault-revealing test data.

The identification of functions in programs can be done by the programmer, assisted by function identification information in requirements and design documentation. Attempts to automate this process by equating functions with program paths or control subpaths have been unsuccessful. Data-flow test coverage can be thought of as the attempt to identify program constructs corresponding to functions by identifying data-flow relationships between statements. If several statements are closely related through the production and use of data, then they are probably part of some intermediate program function and some test should cause the execution of that combination of statements. Two kinds of data-flow coverage, definition-reference and data-context, were discussed, along with a brief description of implementation issues.

In symbolic evaluation, programs (or detailed designs) are executed over symbols standing for data rather than actual data. This results in symbolic expressions that describe the effect of the program over whole classes of data rather than just over single data points. Symbolic evaluation can also be used to generate symbolic systems of predicates that describe the input data that causes program paths to be executed. If a path's system of predicates has no solution, the path is infeasible and no input data will ever cause it to be executed. There is a variety of program analysis methods that involve path traversal which are impractical because of the enormous number of possible paths through a program. Studies indicate that many of a program's paths may be infeasible. The use of symbolic evaluation for infeasible path detection is a potential solution to the difficulties of path-traversal methods. The structure and capabilities of a symbolic evaluation system were described, along with techniques for dealing with programming languages containing nonfunctional operators.

Functional testing depends on being able to verify the output produced for different input tests. The running of a program over test cases and the verification of generated output can be automated using a program test harness. Related to this is the use of dynamic assertions for checking computed values. Dynamic assertions describe invariant properties of intermediate variable values. Code, which checks the assertions during run time, is inserted in a program either manually, or automatically by a dynamic assertion preprocessor.

EXERCISES

5.1. Suppose that path testing is to be used for the *dater* fdl in Figure 3.7, and that all paths up to two-loop iterations are going to be covered. How many such paths are there through *dater*? How many of these are infeasible?

5.2. Repeat Exercise 5.1 for the *covar* fdl in Figure 3.9.

5.3. Identify all of the 1dr- and 2dr-chains in the *dater* fdl in Figure 3.7.

5.4. Identify all of the 1dc- and 2dc-chains in the *dater* fdl in Figure 3.7.

5.5. Identify all of the 1dr- and 2dr-chains in the *covar* fdl in Figure 3.9.

5.6. Identify all of the 1dc- and 2dc-chains in the *covar* fdl in Figure 3.9.

5.7. Symbolically evaluate the paths through the *covar* fdl in Figure 3.9. Evaluate all those paths which do not cause repeated iterations of the loop. Construct symbolic path output like that which was generated for the *dater* fdl in Figure 5.25.

5.8. Suppose that a program's input data consists of a vector v of n elements. Suppose that the elements of v occur according to one probability distribution and n according to another. Extend the hypothesis testing results of Chapter 4 to include this situation. Generalize your result to arbitrary input data structures and variables.

5.9. Identify the requirements, design, and programming functions in several programs ($\simeq$ 100 lines). Attempt to correlate the functions with control- and data-flow coverage measures and assess their accuracy in identifying the functions.

5.10. Design a tool to carry out 2dc-chain testing. Describe the tables to be constructed and the probes that must be inserted by the preprocessor. Discuss the ways in which 2dc-chain testing is more complex or more costly than 2dr-chain testing.

REFERENCES

1. L. G. Stucki, Automatic generation of self-metric software, *Proceedings, IEEE Symposium on Computer Software Reliability*, New York, 1973.
2. J. C. Huang, An approach to program testing, *ACM Computing Surveys*, vol. 7, 1975.
3. W. E. Howden, Methodology for the generation of program test data, *IEEE Transactions on Computers*, vol. C-24, 5, 1975.
4. D. Hedley and M. A. Hennell, The causes and effects of infeasible paths in computer programs, *Proceedings, Eighth International Conference on Software Engineering*, IEEE, Long Beach, 1985.
5. M. R. Woodward, D. Hedley, and M. A. Hennell, Experience with path analysis and testing of programs, *IEEE Transactions on Software Engineering*, vol. 6, 3, May 1980.
6. L. J. Morell and R. G. Hamlet, Error propagation and elimination in computer programs, *University of Maryland TR-1065*, Department of Computer Science, July 1981.
7. S. J. Zeil, Testing for perturbations of program statements, *IEEE Transactions on Software Engineering*, vol. SE-9, 3, 1983.
8. P. M. Herman, A data flow analysis approach to program testing, *The Australian Computer Journal*, vol. 8, 3, 1976.
9. S. C. Ntafos, An evaluation of required element testing strategies, *IEEE Transactions on Software Engineering*, vol. SE-10, 6, November 1984.
10. J. W. Laski and B. Korel, A data flow oriented program testing strategy, *IEEE Transactions on Software Engineering*, vol. SE-9, 3, 1983.
11. S. Rapps and E. J. Weyuker, Data flow analysis techniques for program test data selection, *Proceedings, Sixth International Conference on Software Engineering*, September 1982, pp. 272–278.
12. W. E. Howden, Algebraic program testing, *Acta Informatica*, vol. 10, 1, 1978.
13. W. E. Howden, Lindenmayer grammars and symbolic testing, *Information Processing Letters*, vol. 7, 1, January 1978.
14. W. E. Howden, Symbolic testing and the DISSECT symbolic evaluation system, *IEEE Transactions on Software Engineering*, vol. SE-3, 4, 1977.
15. R. S. Boyer, B. Elspas, and K. N. Levitt, SELECT—A formal system for testing and debugging programs by symbolic execution, *Proceedings, 1975 International Conference on Reliable Software*, IEEE, Long Beach, 1975, pp. 234–245.
16. L. A. Clarke, A system to generate test data and symbolically execute programs, *IEEE Transactions on Software Engineering*, vol. SE-2, 1976.
17. J. C. King, Symbolic execution and program testing, *CACM*, vol. 19, July 1976.
18. M. Ariza, W. E. Howden, I. Miyamoto, M. Nita, and M. Nokugawa, A design for a COBOL symbolic evaluation system (to appear).
19. F. Miller and R. A. Melton, Automated generation of test case data sets, *Proceedings, 1975 International Conference on Reliable Software*, IEEE, Long Beach, 1975, pp. 51–58.

20. K. W. Krause, R. W. Smith, and M. A. Goodwin, Optimal software test planning through automated network analysis, *Proceedings, IEEE Symposium on Computer Software Reliability*, IEEE, 1973, pp. 18–22.

21. L. G. Stucki, New directions in automated tools for improving software quality, in *Current Trends in Programming Methodology*, vol. 2, R. T. Yeh (Ed.), Prentice-Hall, Englewood Cliffs, N.J., 1977, pp. 80–111.

22. D. M. Andrews, A. Mahmood, and E. J. McCluskey, Dynamic assertion testing of flight control software, Stanford University Computer Systems Laboratory, 1985.

CHAPTER

6

FUNCTIONAL ANALYSIS

6.1 INTRODUCTION

Functional testing concentrates on the input-output behavior of individual functions. The principal technique of functional analysis is *structural analysis*. Structural analysis is concerned with the interactions between collections of functions that have been arranged into a program or system structure. The functions may range in complexity from individual statements to large modules. This chapter describes the basic techniques of structural analysis.

Recall that a mistake in a program is called a fault and that the incorrect behavior which is caused by a fault is called a failure. The methods used in functional testing are fault-analysis methods in the sense that they are designed to detect the presence of certain kinds of program faults, such as an expression being off by a constant. A simple fault-analysis method will also be given for structural analysis but most of the methods in this chapter are for performing failure analysis. In failure analysis a description is given of certain kinds of program failures and methods are given for detecting if a program could generate those failures. In structural analysis, failures correspond to incorrect function usage sequences, or incorrect data or function interfaces. Interfaces occur in a variety of ways, the most important of which will be discussed.

Structural analysis depends on different kinds of oracles than those used in functional testing. A *trace oracle* is an oracle which is capable of determining if the sequence of program elements, for example, statements or function calls, occurring along a program path is correct. Trace oracles may also be available for verifying the sequences of states or data types which occur along program paths. Trace oracles are used in the simple structural fault-analysis method that is presented in the following section. However, most of the methods will depend on the use of *interface oracles* for detecting *interface failures* in paths. Interface oracles can be used to determine if an interface between two objects, such as two functions or a function and a data object, is correct in the sense that the interface would also occur during execution of the correct version of the program. Three kinds of interface analysis are discussed: module, operator, and data interface analysis.

Structural analysis can be applied to both programs and to the fdl algorithms in detailed designs.

6.2 TRACE-FAULT ANALYSIS

Different kinds of flow graphs G can be derived from a program P, corresponding to different kinds of trace-fault analysis. In all cases G has the same graph structure and it is only the information at the nodes and arcs of G which differs. In *statement trace-fault analysis* each node in G is associated with a statement in P. If the statement is conditional, then the arcs coming out of the node will be labeled with the statement's branch conditions. Trace-fault analysis in this case involves verifying the correctness of the sequences of statements and branch conditions which occur along program paths and depends on the use of a statement or branch sequence oracle.

If a program is commented with state or type descriptions, then a flow graph whose nodes are associated with state or type comments can be constructed. If a state or type sequence oracle is available, then sequence analysis can be used to detect state or type sequence faults.

It is often reasonable to assume for statement- or state-flow graphs that the paths through the graphs will be distinct. Otherwise the program would be redundant in some sense. This means that no two paths will have the same sequence of statements or state descriptions. Under this assumption, Theorem 4.37 in Chapter 4 indicates that trace analysis can be used to detect faults in which a statement or state has been omitted. The theorem specifies that what is required is to examine all paths through the program which traverse no statement (or state) more than twice. Additional research on trace analysis should result in the characterization of more complex classes of faults which trace analysis is capable of detecting, including those which result in some of the interface failures described in the following sections.

6.3 INTERFACE FAILURE ANALYSIS

Omission of statements is a very simple kind of structural fault. More complex structural faults include, for example, the failure to subordinate one conditional statement to another. Consider the two flow graphs in Figure 6.1. The one on the left corresponds to a program P in which one conditional branching statement is nested inside the other. The diagram on the right corresponds to a slightly different program in which the two statements appear in sequence, without any nesting. The labels $a, b, c,$ and d correspond to operations which are executed as a result of the conditional selection.

One of the characteristic features of structural faults like that illustrated in Figure 6.1 is that they result in the unexpected interfacing of two program elements. In the diagram on the left operation a does not interface with any of the other operations in the sense that it is not immediately followed by one of them. On the right, operation a is always followed by either c or d. If it is incorrect, for example, for a not to be the last operation in a sequence, then the program corresponding to the diagram on the right contains an interface fault. Operation a illegally interfaces with other operations. There is a very wide class of situations like this for which *interface oracles* exist which can be used to determine the legality of the interfaces in a program, and hence the occurrence of interface failure-causing structural faults.

6.4 MODULE-INTERFACE ANALYSIS

The first kind of interface analysis that will be described analyzes interfaces between program or system modules. A *module* is defined to be a part of a system which is identified with a unique name and which is encapsulated using a standard construct. The simplest common kind of module is a function, subroutine, or procedure. Its *calling interface* consists of its name and its formal parameter list. A subroutine may contain *caller interfaces*. These are calls to other subroutines and consist of a subroutine name and an actual parameter list.

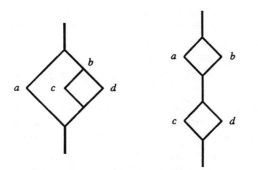

FIGURE 6.1. Conditional statement subordination fault.

Modules may contain more than one function (or subroutine or procedure). These functions may interact either with other functions in the same module or with functions in other modules. The calling interface for a module containing more than one function consists of the calling interfaces for each function which can be called by a function from outside the module. Its caller interface consists of the caller interfaces of the functions in the module that involve calls on functions in other modules.

The interface between two modules M and N consists of the calls of functions in M on functions in N and/or the calls in N on functions in M. Module-interface analysis is the examination of the consistency of the calling interfaces of the functions in one module with the associated caller interfaces of functions in the other. If a function in module M calls a function in module N, then the actual parameter list of the call in M is compared with the formal parameter list in N. They can be compared to see that they have the same number of parameters and that corresponding parameters are of the same type.

In addition to inconsistency, module-interface analysis can be used to detect incompleteness and redundancy. Incompleteness occurs when a function is called which is not defined and redundancy occurs when a function is defined in some module but is never used by any other function in that or other modules.

Techniques and supporting tools for defining modules, and for module-interface analysis, have been in use for a number of years and have been reported to be effective.[1]

6.5 INTERFACE ANALYSIS OF DATA STRUCTURE OPERATIONS

Module-interface analysis examines interfaces between the largest or highest-level functional objects in a system. Operator-interface analysis examines the interfaces between low-level functional objects, the operators that are used to access data structures.

Data structures of a particular type will have one or more operators associated with them which are used for accessing the data structure. Stacks, for example, are accessed using the operators *push* and *pop*. Other examples include the *read, write, open*, and *close* operations for files. The referencing of and assignment to a variable can also be thought of as very simple examples of operators.

In some programs, variables may be used in a special way to simulate a data structure, and the operators in the program may not be explicit operators in the programming language, or even separately defined functions. For the purpose of structural program analysis the programmer can insert comments which identify the operators. Suppose, for example, that a simple variable *lastaccount* is used to detect account breaks in a file-processing application. Each time a new record is read by the program, *lastaccount* will be used to determine if a new account is being processed by comparing the account numbers of the new account and last account. After the check, *lastaccount* can be updated to the (possibly) new account number. The two basic operators used for the *lastaccount* break-check data structure are *checkbreak* and *updatebreak*. It is unlikely that these will be explicit operators in any programming language. Comments can be used to identify the code which corresponds to instances of these operators.

There are two kinds of analysis techniques for data structure operations: type checking and operator-sequence analysis. Type checking is used to make sure that operators are applied to the right kinds of data structures. Operator-sequence analysis involves multiple interacting data operators. It is used to confirm that interacting operators have not been applied in illegal sequences.

Type checking for correct usage of data operators can be more formally defined using abstract data types. Recall that data types can be characterized by describing the properties of the operations that can be performed on them. Figure 6.2 reproduces the abstract data type definition for integer stacks which was introduced in Chapter 3. Figure 6.3 contains another example, in which a particular kind of array index is defined. It defines an *aindex* to be an integer in the range 1, 2,..., 100 which can be added to and subtracted from *aindex*'s. The axioms in the *aindex* definition describe the important properties of the *aindex* data operations. In order to use types of data like those described in Figures 6.2 and 6.3, it is necessary to map them onto programming language structures and operations. Some advanced programming languages allow the description of user-defined types, as well as having a variety of built-in types similar to those in the more common languages. For user-defined types, the programmer must write the code that implements the type's operators. For built-in types, the programmer declares objects to be of a certain type and uses the built-in implementations of the type's operators. In either case, a type checker can be used which will ensure that no operator (i.e., the code implementing an operator) is applied to the wrong type of data (i.e., to a variable or data structure which has been declared as being used to hold data of the wrong type).

type:	*intstack*
sorts:	*intstack, integer*
uses:	*integers*
operators:	*push(integer,intstack)* → *intstack*
	pop(intstack) → *intstack*
	top(intstack) → *integer*
axioms:	*pop(push(x,s))* → *s*
	top(push(x,s)) → *x*

FIGURE 6.2.   Type definition for integer stack.

type: *aindex*
sorts: *aindex, error, integers*
uses: *integers*
operators: *indexadd(aindex,aindex)* $\rightarrow$ *aindex* $\bigvee$ *error*
                 indexsub(aindex,aindex) $\rightarrow$ *aindex* $\bigvee$ *error*
axioms: *indexadd(x,y)* = if $x + y \leq 100$ then $x + y$
                               else "*overflow*"
                 indexsub(x,y) = if $x - y \geq 1$ then $x - y$
                               else "*underflow*"

FIGURE 6.3.   Type definition for an array index.

A critical feature of the operators associated with data structures is that they should only be used in certain sequences. Different techniques can be used to distinguish between legal and illegal sequences. One approach is to use graphs in which operators are associated with nodes. Legal operator sequences correspond to paths through a legal sequences graph. Figure 6.4 contains a sample diagram for the four file manipulation operators *read*, *write*, *open*, and *close*. Starting nodes in legal sequences flow graphs will be denoted with a small circle. Legal sequences diagrams may have one or more terminal nodes which are designated with a black dot. Legal sequences must begin with the start node and end on a terminal node.

Figure 6.4 specifies that the first file operation for a file must be an *open*. This can be followed by any mixture of *read* and *write* operations, and then a final *close* must occur.

Perhaps the simplest sequence specification is that for variable assignment and referencing. This is described by the diagram in Figure 6.5. It is the basis for static-analysis techniques in which a program is examined for references to uninitialized variables.

If it is considered illegal to assign a value which is not subsequently referenced, then the diagram in Figure 6.6 can be used.

Simple graphs cannot be used to distinguish between the same variety of legal and illegal operator sequences as other techniques. They cannot be used, for example, to specify that the number of *pops* from a stack must be

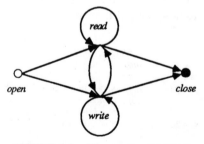

FIGURE 6.4.   File operator sequences.

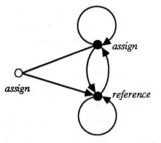

FIGURE 6.5. Legal sequences of assign and reference.

equal to the number of preceding *pushes*. But they are usually more than sufficient.

In order to determine if the operator sequences in a program are legal or are contained in a legal sequences graph, it is normally necessary only to compare pairs of adjacent operators. Two operators *f* and *g* in a program are adjacent if there is a subpath from *f* to *g* containing no other operators. The reason why it is necessary only to compare adjacent operator pairs is that legal operator sequence diagrams can be expected to have the Markov property. Recall that the Markov property means that all occurrences of any given operator in a graph are followed by the same set of operators. Theorem 4.38 from Chapter 4 proves that if a legal sequences graph has the Markov property and if all adjacent pairs in a program are adjacent pairs in the graph, then every node path in the program is a node path in the graph. It is then necessary only to make sure that the start and termination nodes of a path's node sequence in the program are start and termination nodes in the graph.

Operators in a program may be explicit if they are features in the programming language used, or correspond to explicitly defined functions or routines having the same names. Assignments and references to variables can be considered to be explicit, corresponding to the assignment and reference operations of the language. When the occurrence of an operator does not correspond to an explicit function or other programming language feature, then its presence can be denoted with a functional comment of the form

    {operatorname}   or   *{operatorname dataname}*

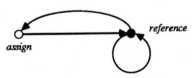

FIGURE 6.6. Legal sequences where references must be used.

where the name of the operator is listed, or in the case where the same name is used for operators which are computationally equivalent but used with different variables or data structures, the name of both the operator and the data object.

Variables and data structures are usually assigned values and referenced with explicit operations. What is not usually explicit is when they become undefined, or when their data is no longer correct and should not be used until reset. Consider the example in Figure 6.7, in which a *count* variable is initialized and then updated inside a nested loop. When the nested loop is exited, the *count* contents are printed, after which it is considered to be a no longer available data item, until it is reinitialized and then recomputed. This is indicated with a comment indicating an implicit *cancel* operator which "undefines" the contents of *count*.

Operator-sequence analysis can be carried out using the label-pairs (lp) traversal algorithm introduced in Section 4.8. Recall that in that algorithm graph nodes have labels (some may not) and the algorithm generates all pairs (a,b) where a and b are the labels on two nodes (n_1, n_2) connected by a label-free subpath. The algorithm is applied to a program by treating statements as graph nodes, and if a statement involves an operator, labeling its graph node with that operator. The lp traversal algorithm can be augmented to detect path start and termination nodes.

It should be noted that if an operator pair (f,g) is connected by an infeasible subpath, or a subpath of an infeasible path, then the execution of f followed by g never actually happens. If the legal-sequences graph does not contain an operator interface (f,g), it would be a mistake to report that the program has an operator interface problem. It may be possible to avoid this using infeasible-path analysis.

Operator-interface analysis has been found to be a very powerful error-detection method. A relatively large percentage of many of the different kinds of structural faults that can occur in a program result in very simple interface failures. In the study of 100 program errors reported by Howden,[2] 12

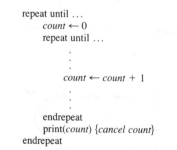

FIGURE 6.7.   Implicit "undefine" operator.

were found to be detectable by assignment/reference interface analysis alone. In a study of the later versions of a 100,000 line COBOL general ledger accounting system, persistent, missing code errors invariably resulted in some form of operator-interface error detectable using operator-interface analysis.

In summary, the application of operator-sequence analysis has three steps:

1. Specify all data operators and their legal sequencing;
2. Identify the data operators in the program, possibly using program comments, and use a program traverser to generate all operator pairs; and
3. Check program operator pairs against legal sequencing information.

The analysis must be carried out separately for each set of interacting operators for each data structure. This implies, for example, that assignment-reference analysis must be carried out separately for each variable. The legal-sequencing analysis of file operations must be carried out separately for each file. Fortunately, these separate analyses can be carried out in parallel so that the lp traverser would have to be applied only once. The traverser would be used in such a way that it generated operator pairs for each of the different sets of operators currently under analysis, and these would be checked against the appropriate legal operator sequences definitions.

Although static analysis for uninitialized variables is well known, there are no general purpose operator-interface analysis systems that are widely available.

6.6 DATA-INTERFACE ANALYSIS

6.6.1 Data Transformations

Module-interface analysis is applied to "large" objects that occur at the higher levels of abstraction of a system's description. The modules and their interfaces may be developed during design and the analysis carried out at that stage of system development. Operator analysis and type checking are applied to "small" objects that occur at the lowest level of detail, that of accessing and using data structures. What they both have in common is that they analyze interfaces between explicitly defined functional objects. Programs also contain interfaces at intermediate levels between these two, interfaces that do not correspond to explicitly declared functions.

If a program is viewed as something which carries data through a sequence of data transformations from an initial type, through intermediate types and flavors, to a final type, then it can be thought of as containing internal interfaces that occur between transformations. These internal transformations take place as control passes from one statement to another, or out along a branch from a conditional branching statement. Since there may be no explicit functions involved, the interfaces are described in terms of the types of data produced and used along program paths.

The correct flow of data, as it is transformed from one type to another, can be modeled using a data-flow diagram in much the same way that legal operator sequences graphs were used to describe legal sequences of data structure operations. A diagram similar to that used for specifying the data-flow requirements for a system can be used except that only the data, and not the data transformations, need be included. Figure 6.8 reproduces the data-type diagram for the dating system which was introduced in Section 3.4.1.

Figure 6.8 specifies that *daterequest* type data together with *datefile* type data be transformed into *clientinfo* type data. Then *clientinfo* and *dateinfo* types of data are transformed into *score* data, which is finally transformed into *bestmatch* data.

6.6.2   Sufficiency of Data-Interface Analysis

Data-flow analysis requires a list of types of interest for a program or fdl, as well as a data-flow diagram that describes the correct sequences of data transformations for these types. The program is analyzed to see if the sequences of data transformations involving types in the list of types of interest are contained in the data-flow specification. Since the number of paths through a program can grow exponentially in the number of program statements, comparisons of all possible program data-flow paths with data-flow diagram data transformation sequences are potentially very expensive. Fortunately, most data-flow diagrams have properties that make it possible, as in operator-sequence analysis, to have to do only interface analysis.

In data-interface analysis, a program is analyzed to see if its data interfaces occur in an associated specifications data-flow graph. A data interface is a structure

$$(a_1, a_2, \ldots, a_n) \to b$$

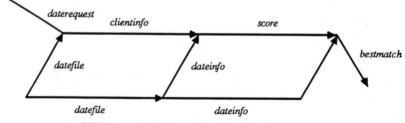

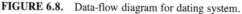

FIGURE 6.8.   Data-flow diagram for dating system.

where the types $a_1, a_2, \ldots, a_n$ are used to produce a new type b. The simplest example of this would be an assignment statement in which b is the type of data which occurs at the left of the assignment and $a_1, a_2, \ldots, a_n$ are the types of data which occur on the right. The conditions for the sufficiency of interface analysis are defined in Theorem 4.39. Recall that this theorem states the following. If G and G' are two data-flow diagrams (graphs with labeled arcs), and if G' has completely duplicated labels, and if all of the interfaces in G are interfaces in G', then G is a subgraph of G' (i.e., the data flow modeled by G is contained in G').

The completely duplicated labels condition requires that if there is a data flow of type a from n_1 to n_2 and also from m_1 to m_2, then there is also one from n_1 to m_2. This is an intuitively meaningful requirement since what it means is that if data of some particular type is produced somewhere in a data-flow diagram, then it is available for use by all data transformations that use that kind of data. Or, put the other way, if data of a particular type is used by some data transformation, then it can use all instances of that data in the data-flow graph. If a data item d is produced by some data transformation in the data-flow graph (i.e., there is an arc coming out of a node n_1 with a data type label d on it), but is not available for use by some other data transformation which uses that kind of data (i.e., there is another node n_2 with an arc coming into it with data d, but no arc from n_1 to n_2 with data d), then in some sense the same kind of data is being treated differently at two different places in the data-flow diagram and two new kinds of data, say subtypes d_1 and d_2, should be created. The completely duplicated labels property means that all data of the same type should be treated the same.

If all of the data interfaces in a program P are contained in the legal type interface data-flow diagram L for P, and if L has completely duplicated labels, then the flow of data through P will be contained in L. It is also necessary to check that the input and output data flows in P are input and output data flows in L. An *input data flow* is a data-flow arc which comes from an input data-flow node having no input data-flow arcs. An *output data flow* is a data-flow arc which flows into an output data-flow node having no data-flow arcs coming out of it. The interface data-flow analysis process can be constructed to check not only that interfaces in P are in L but that an interface is an input or output interface in P if and only if it is an input or output interface in L.

All of the data-flow graphs in the following examples have the completely duplicated labels condition. The only exception to this is the case where there is more than one input node which generates the same kind of input data flow. This is not a problem since all such input nodes can be considered to be the same node, and the separation into different nodes is only a convenience for drawing the data-flow diagram.

The construction of a specifications data-flow diagram describing legal data-flow interfaces and sequences can occur during requirements or design, but the method is still useful even if the diagram is constructed after the fact, after implementation. This is not meant to imply that it should be constructed from the program. It must still be constructed from the user's independent understanding of what correct data-flow patterns look like, since it must be a source of information independent of the program. For interface analysis, it is not necessary to have a complete data-flow diagram. Only the pairs of legal data interfaces are needed. But it is often much easier for the programmer/designer to describe his understanding of the correct data flow in a data-flow diagram rather than a list of pairs, so that the use of complete diagrams will be assumed.

To carry out an interface analysis of a program it is necessary to identify instances of the types of interest in a program and to generate all interfaces between these types. The identification of data types in a program and their interfaces must be capable of being done with minimal effort on the part of the programmer. If it is necessary to manually construct a complete list of interfaces from the program in order to compare its data interfaces with those in the specifications data-flow diagram, then it is less likely that the method will be used. Fortunately, the recognition of program data types and flavors and their interfaces can be at least partially automated.

6.6.3 Identification of Data Types and Type Interfaces

The types and flavors of data which occur in a program can be identified in a variety of ways. If the programming language being used contains facilities for the definition of data types, then type declarations can be examined. In conventional programming languages, where type declarations do not exist or are limited, the occurrence of different types of data and different flavors can be identified using variable names and type comments. It is considered good programming practice to give names to variables which describe the purpose of the variable (mnemonic names). This can be done by giving them names corresponding to the type of data stored in them. In the fdl for the *dater* function, for example, the *clientinfo, bscore,* and *bdate* variables all have names which describe the kinds of data they store.

When a variable can contain different types of data, that is, when flavors occur, then the programmer needs to insert type comments like those described in Chapter 3. Recall that a simple comment of the form

$$\{x \text{ is } typea\}$$

was suggested, where x is a variable name and *typea* a data type name. In the fdl for the *covar* subroutine, for example, the variable *vcv* can at different times contain *unadjustedcrossproducts, adjustedcrossproducts,* and *variancecovariance* types of data.

In the *covar* example, the type of the data stored in *vcv* is changed by assignment statements. Another important place where the type of data that is stored in a variable changes is after the conditional test in a conditional branching statement. Suppose a program contains a statement of the form

$$\text{if } x < 0 \text{ then } y \leftarrow x \text{ else } z \leftarrow x.$$

If the then branch is taken, then it is known that x is negative. Suppose that this corresponds to a type of data known to the programmer as *typeneg*, and that the complementary type associated with the else branch is known as *typenonneg*. This information could be inserted in the program with type classification comments. For this example they would look like:

$$\text{if } x < 0 \text{ then } \{x \text{ is typeneg}\}$$
$$y \leftarrow x$$
$$\text{else } \{x \text{ is typenonneg}\}$$
$$z \leftarrow x.$$

Note that a type comment in a conditional statement is "in force" only if the associated branch is taken in the statement.

In addition to the two basic methods for type recognition—variable names and type comments—there are several other methods that are variations on these ideas and will be discussed later.

The most fundamental kind of data transformation interface is that which is established by an assignment statement. Suppose that a program contains an assignment of the form

$$x \leftarrow y$$

where x and y are known to be of type *typea* and *typeb*. Then there is a data interface established between *typea* and *typeb* which will be denoted as follows, using an arrow which goes in the opposite direction to that of an assignment arrow. The notation indicates that *typeb* data is used to generate *typea* data.

$$typeb \rightarrow typea$$

If the right-hand side of an assignment has more than one variable, then a data interface has occurred in which several types of data interface with another type.

Another very basic kind of data type transformation occurs when a conditional statement is executed. There is an interface between what the type of the data was known to be before the condition evaluation and what it is known to be after the evaluation. In general, a classification comment must be used to give a name to the type after the evaluation if an interface is to be generated. Suppose a construct like that in Figure 6.9 occurs in a program, and the type of x is *typex* before execution of the statement. Assume if *exp(x)*   then {*x is typea*}

...

else {*x is typeb*}

...

FIGURE 6.9.   Conditional comment type interfaces.

that *exp(x)* is some expression containing *x*. Then the comments allow the identification of the type interface

$$typex \rightarrow typea$$

associated with the then branch, and the interface

$$typex \rightarrow typeb$$

associated with the else branch. The comment has the additional effect that subsequent references to *x* in the then and else parts of the if statement are interpreted as references to *typea* or *typeb* data and not *typex* data.

Comments associated with assignment statements will also result in the identification of a type interface. Suppose a program contains an assignment of the form

$$x \leftarrow exp(y) \ \{x \ is \ typea\}$$

where *exp(y)* is an expression in *y*. Then normally, if the type of *x* were just its name *x*, an assignment interface

$$y \rightarrow x$$

would be generated. Because of the comment, an additional interface

$$x \rightarrow typea$$

occurs, and all references to *x* after the assignment are considered to be references to *typea* data.

Comments about variables on the right-hand side of an assignment also result in the identification of type interfaces. Suppose, for example, that the type of a variable is its name *y* before the assignment:

$$x \leftarrow exp(y) \qquad \{y \ is \ typeb\}.$$

Then two interfaces can be identified:

$$y \rightarrow typeb \quad and \quad typeb \rightarrow x.$$

As stated previously, after the type comment the type of data in *y* will be the comment type, *typeb*, and all references to *y* will be assumed to be references to *typeb* data.

In review, the two basic ways of identifying types in a program are to interpret variable names as types and to use type comments. The two basic kinds of type interfaces are those that occur when an assignment is carried out or when a conditional statement branch is followed. In the case of conditional statements, type classification comments are needed to give a new name to the type of data in a variable after it is known to satisfy (or not satisfy) some condition. Comments can also be used to specify a new type for a variable after an assignment. If the name of a variable signifies the type of data stored in it, then type comments can be thought of as a way of (possibly temporarily) changing the name of the variable.

In addition to the type interfaces described, there are other kinds of interfaces which are more closely associated with the programming or fdl language used to describe an algorithm. The ones that occur in the dating and *covar* fdl examples will be described. They are generated by function and subroutine calls.

When a subroutine call occurs in a program there is an implied data interface between the input and output parameters for the subroutine. In order for these interfaces to be documented it is necessary to include input and output comments which specify which parameters are input or output (or both). This can be done with comments of the form:

$$\{input: temp(i)\}$$
$$\{output: mean\}$$

which would result in the generation of a data interface:

$$temp(i) \rightarrow mean.$$

If a variable is both input and output, a type comment can be used to identify the new type of the variable after the subroutine call, as in:

$$\{input: vcv,m\}$$
$$\{output: vcv\}$$
$$transformacptovcv(vcv,m)$$
$$\{vcv \ is \ variancecovariance\}$$

If, say, *adjustedcrossproducts* and *mean* were the types of *vcv* and *m* before the subroutine call, then the result would be the generation of the type interfaces:

$$(adjustedcrossproducts, mean) \rightarrow vcv \qquad and \qquad vcv \rightarrow variancecovariance.$$

There are also a number of special rules associated with function calls in functional fdl's. Two uses of functions will be analyzed: functions as variables and functions as input devices.

In standard functional programming notation, the value returned by a function call is associated with the function name. In the same way that a variable's name is used to denote the type of data stored in the variable, the name of a function can be used to designate the type of data returned by the function. Suppose that a program or fdl contains the assignment:

$$x \leftarrow f(y).$$

This implies that y is used to compute the value of f which is then used to give a value to x. If the names of x and y are used to designate the type of data stored in them, then the assignment generates the following type interfaces:

$$y \rightarrow f \quad \text{and} \quad f \rightarrow x.$$

Comments can be used to change the name of the type returned by the function so that the construct

$$x \leftarrow f(y) \quad \{f \text{ is typea}\}$$

will generate the interfaces

$$y \rightarrow f \quad f \rightarrow typea \quad typea \rightarrow x.$$

Recall that functions appearing on the left-hand side of an assignment in a functional fdl may denote parts of data structures. If x and y have the types of their names, then

$$f(x) \leftarrow y$$

will generate the interface

$$y \rightarrow x$$

since x is the type of data included and f is only the access function.

If a function contains a return statement, this will have the effect of assigning a value to the function. A functional fdl allows the user to return the values of a selected set of variables or data structures. Suppose that x and y have the types of their names and a function f contains the statement:

$$\text{return}(x,y).$$

This will result in the generation of an interface:

$$(x,y) \rightarrow f.$$

In fdl's, functions are used to stand for input devices or files so that the interpretation of the assignment

$$clmessage \leftarrow getdt \ (clientid)$$

in terms of the interfaces

$$clientid \rightarrow getdt \quad \text{and} \quad getdt \rightarrow clmessage$$

may be inadequate. This problem is solved with an additional comment of the form:

$$\{f \ uses \ devicename\}.$$

This comment says that f depends on *devicename* in addition to any input variables it may have. Suppose, in the given example, *getdt* is a function that returns records from a database called *datefile*. Then this could be designated with:

$$clmessage \leftarrow getdt(clientid) \ \{getdt \ uses \ datefile\}.$$

The occurrence of this construct in a program will result in the data interfaces:

$$(datefile, clientid) \rightarrow getdt \quad \text{and} \quad getdt \rightarrow clmessage.$$

Several conventions can be used to simplify the data-interface information generated by a data-interface analyzer. The first is that constants will not be considered types of data, so that an assignment statement of the form

$$x \leftarrow 6,$$

for example, will not result in the generation of any data interface. In the case where constants are mixed with types, they will also be ignored so that an assignment of the form

$$x \leftarrow 6 + y + z$$

will result in the interface

$$(y, z) \rightarrow x.$$

Redundant type interfaces can also be eliminated. Suppose that the assignment

$$x \leftarrow x+1$$

occurs in a program. Normally this might result in the redundant interface

$$x \rightarrow x.$$

Such interfaces are discarded.

The specifications data-flow diagrams used in data-interface analysis may be significantly less detailed than the program or fdl to be analyzed, so that the analysis of a program or fdl may result in the generation of data interfaces not included in the data-flow specification. This can be partly avoided by supplying the program analyzer with a list of types of interest as mentioned earlier. The list can be prepared from the data-flow specification or a list of type interfaces. The analyzer, in constructing type interfaces from the program, uses the list to perform *type compression*. Suppose, for example, that the following two type interfaces occur in a program:

$$typea \rightarrow typeb \quad \text{and} \quad typeb \rightarrow typec$$

and that the types-of-interest type list contains only the types *typea* and *typec*. Then an analyzer capable of type compression will produce only the interface

$$typea \rightarrow typec.$$

When a types-of-interest list is used, only those interfaces containing types in the list will be generated during interface analysis. A possible exception is when a type not in the list occurs on the left side of an interface. In this case there may be an unassigned input fault, assuming that the types of all input data are in the types-of-interest list, and it may be useful to generate information about the interface and its unassigned input.

6.6.4   Generation of Data-Type Interfaces

Path-traversal algorithms like those described in Chapter 4 can be used to implement data-interface analysis. A data-interface tool will have to include a preprocessor phase which puts the program into a traversable flow-graph format. The preprocessed program (or fdl) will have to include all the relevant information about types and embedded comments. Transfers of control into, within, and out of conditional statements will have to be carefully distinguished so that temporary new type names associated with conditional selection can be generated and cancelled at the appropriate places.

Data-interface analysis examines assignment, conditional, input-output, and subroutine or function call statements, but it does not examine loop or iteration constructs. This is because the iteration control in a program does not, in theory, involve the generation of new types of data. If a conditional branching statement is used for loop control, rather than data type discrimination, it may result in spurious data interfaces, spurious in the sense that they will not appear in the data-flow specification. This implies that good data-flow analysis requires good programs, and one of the possible implications of a detected data-interface problem is that the program should be rewritten.

The path-traversal process required for data-flow analysis will have to carry along three kinds of information as it traverses program paths. The first are type redefinitions. Whenever a comment is encountered in which a variable is assigned a type, this information is put in the type redefinitions list. When a reference to a variable occurs, the redefinitions list must be accessed to see if it has a type specified by a comment. If not, its name is used. If a type redefinition is made for a variable already having a type redefinition in the list, the old entry is deleted when the new one is added.

The second kind of information consists of the conditional types. Suppose that a variable occurs in the condition for a conditional branching statement. Then its type interfaces with the types of all variables receiving values in the then and else parts of the statement. This is because it is part of the types used to determine the new values for the variables. When the scope of an if statement is left during path traversal, the associated entries in the conditional types list must be deleted. In the following if statement, for example, the variable *word* determines whether or not *telegramwordcount* gets a new value:

> if *special(word)* = *false*
> then *telegramwordcount* ← *telegramwordcount* + 1.

Hence the interface

$$word \rightarrow telegramwordcount$$

is generated. If there is a type redefinitions comment, as in

> if *special(word)* = *false*
> then {*word is notspecialword*}
>   *telegramwordcount* ← *telegramwordcount* + 1

and the then branch in the statement is followed, then the interfaces

word → *notspecial word*   and   *notspecialword* → *telegramwordcount*

will be generated and the type redefinition

$$word = notspecialword$$

added to the type redefinitions list. An even more complex situation can occur when a variable already has a type redefinition before the encounter of an if statement. Suppose that *word* has had its type redefined as *oversizeword* on the path leading up to the above if statement, and the then branch is selected. Then the interfaces

$$oversizeword \rightarrow notspecialword$$

and   *notspecialword* → *telegramwordcount*

will occur.

In a complex structure having nested if statements with compound (multistatement) then/else clauses, the types of the variables in the condition, or the redefined types, will have to be carried along any path through the conditional structure up to the point where control exits from it.

The third kind of information that needs to be carried along during program analysis is the information needed to do type compression. Assume that the data-interface analyzer has been supplied with a list of types of interest, and suppose that it maintains a current uncompressed interfaces list. This will be a list of interfaces $x \rightarrow y$ where either x or y, or both, are types not on the types of interest list. Suppose that a statement is reached and a new data-type interface is generated. Then the list is searched to see if compression should occur and/or a new interface should be added to the list.

The rules for type compression are quite simple. Suppose that an interface of the form

$$(y_1, y_2, \ldots, y_n) \rightarrow x$$

occurs in a statement. Then, if it is assumed that every input variable is in the interest list, either y_i, $1 \leq i \leq n$, is in the interest list or there must be interfaces of the form

$$(z_1, z_2, \ldots, z_n) \rightarrow y_i$$

in the current uncompressed interfaces list, where each z_i is in the interest list. Substitute $z_1, z_2, \ldots, z_n$ for each y_i which is not in the interest list to get an interface,

$$(w_1, w_2, \ldots, w_t) \rightarrow x$$

where each w_i is in the interest list. Now if x is also in the interest list, output the interface. Otherwise, put the interface in the current uncompressed interfaces list.

A situation that demands extra care occurs when a comment of the form

$$\{x \text{ is typeb}\}$$

occurs for a variable for which there is already a type redefinition, say, *typea*. Recall that the comment will generate an interface

$$typea \rightarrow typeb$$

since x is currently known as *typea*. It is important to generate the interface before changing x's type redefinition to *typeb*, otherwise an interface

$$typeb \rightarrow typeb$$

will be erroneously generated.

The dynamic labels (dl) path traversal algorithm described in Section 4.8 of Chapter 4 can be used to implement a data-interfaces analyzer. Recall that in the algorithm, each node of a flow graph is associated with label operators which may add or delete labels from the current label set. The traversal process terminates its traversal of a path if it reaches a node with a current label set that is the same as a previous current label set reaching the node. Theorem 4.35 proves that the algorithm will construct all label sets that could occur during any possible traversal of the flow graph.

In the application of dl to data-interface analysis, flow-graph nodes are associated with program statements. Labels are associated with type-redefinition lists, conditional-type lists, and uncompressed data-interface lists. The label generation and cancellation operators associated with a node are the operations which add and delete type redefinitions, conditional types, and uncompressed data interfaces. The algorithm is modified to output or generate a data-interface pair whenever one is encountered in which both the input and output data types are in the types-of-interest list. It is also modified to check that input or output data-flow arcs generated by the program are also input or output arcs in the specification or legal sequences data-flow diagram.

The interfaces generated during dl traversal are thought of as being part of an implicit data-flow diagram in the program or fdl under analysis. If all of the interfaces in a program P are interfaces in a legal sequences data-flow diagram L for P, then the implicit program data-flow diagram is a subgraph of L. Hence, all data-flow sequences in P are contained in L, and the program contains no data-flow sequence faults.

The use of data-flow diagrams for type-interface analysis has also been investigated by Werner.[3]

The following section contains examples of the application of operator- and data-interface analysis to the fdl detailed designs for the *covar* and dating system examples.

6.7 OPERATOR- AND DATA-INTERFACE ANALYSIS EXAMPLES

6.7.1 Dating System Example

The fdl for the dating system *dater* function is reproduced in Figure 6.10. Comments have been included to clarify the types of data stored in variables and returned by functions. Note that no comment is included for the

```
function dater(daterequest)
     clientid ← id(daterequest)
     clmessage ← getdt(clientid) {getdt uses datefile}
     if nocl(clmessage) ≠ nil
          then return ("error: no such daterclient")
     clientinfo ← info(clmessage)
     bscore ← 0
     initializedtfile
     repeat while not(enddtfile)
          dateinfo ← getnextdt {getnextdt uses datefile}
          score ← blissf(clientinfo,dateinfo)
          if score > bscore
               then bscore ← score
                    bdate ← dateinfo
     endrepeat
     {bdate is bestmatch}
     return(bdate)
endfunction
```

FIGURE 6.10.   Fdl *dater* function with data types.

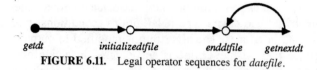

getdt   *initializedtfile*   *enddtfile*   *getnextdt*

FIGURE 6.11.   Legal operator sequences for *datefile*.

branches of the conditional statement comparing *score* with *bscore*. This is because the type change resulting from the test is described by the assignment following the branch and no comment is necessary.

The fdl for *dater* includes the file operations *getdt*, *initializedtfile*, *getnextdt*, and *enddtfile*. Recall that in this application, the *getdt* random access operator is to be applied first, before sequential processing of the file. In any legal operators sequence, it should come first, followed by an *initializedtfile* operation which sets up the file for sequential access. Before each sequential access, the *enddtfile* operator must be used to check that there are still more records in the file. The set of all legal operator sequences is described by the diagram in Figure 6.11. The *dater* fdl can be easily analyzed for legality of usage of the *datefile* operators.

Figure 6.12 reproduces from Figure 6.8 the data-flow specification for *dater*. If the data-interface analysis procedure is applied to *dater* without data compression, then the data interfaces in Figure 6.13 will be produced. The only interface listed in Figure 6.13 that might not be completely obvious is

clmessage → *dater*.

This is generated by the

return *("error: no such daterclient")*

statement. Recall that return acts like an assignment statement which assigns a value to the function *dater*. Since the return is within the scope of the conditional, an interface

(clmessage, "error: no such daterclient") → *dater*

is implied. Since the second element of the pair on the left is a constant and not a type of data, it is dropped.

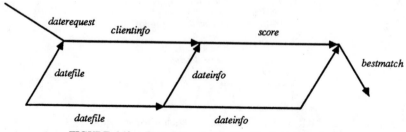

FIGURE 6.12.   Data-flow specification for dating function.

$$\underline{daterequest} \rightarrow id$$
$$\underline{id} \rightarrow clientid$$
$$(clientid,\underline{datefile}) \rightarrow getdt$$
$$getdt \rightarrow clmessage$$
$$clmessage \rightarrow dater$$
$$clmessage \rightarrow info$$
$$info \rightarrow \underline{clientinfo}$$
$$\underline{datefile} \rightarrow getnextdt$$
$$getnextdt \rightarrow \underline{dateinfo}$$
$$(\underline{clientinfo},\underline{dateinfo}) \rightarrow blissf$$
$$blissf \rightarrow \underline{score}$$
$$\underline{score} \rightarrow bscore$$
$$(\underline{dateinfo},\underline{score},bscore) \rightarrow bdate$$
$$bdate \rightarrow \underline{bestmatch}$$
$$\underline{bestmatch} \rightarrow dater$$

FIGURE 6.13. Uncompressed data interfaces for *dater*.

If the types in the data specifications diagram are assumed to compose the types-of-interest list and type compression is used, then the data interfaces in Figure 6.14 will be generated. The types of interest in the specifications diagram are underlined in the uncompressed interfaces in Figure 6.13.

Comparison of the interfaces from the fdl with those occurring in the data-flow specification indicates data interface consistency.

6.7.2 *covar* Example

The fdl for *covar* is reproduced in Figure 6.15. Comments have been included to show the input and output parameters for the subroutine calls and for the renamed types of the data stored in the output variables. In actual practice the programmer would probably want to include more, and slightly different, type comments, including a complete set for the program's input variables. This set was chosen partly for space considerations. The same type interface analysis would result for the more detailed set. In the example, the convention was used that the type of an array element is the type of the whole array unless it is explicitly defined to be something else.

Figure 6.16 contains the specifications data-flow diagram for *covar* and Figure 6.17 the compressed data interfaces generated from the *covar* fdl. Comparison of the list of interfaces with the data-flow diagram interfaces indicates that *covar* has no data interface errors.

In both the *dater* and *covar* examples, no faults are found using operator- or data-interface analysis. In order to illustrate the use of these methods in finding faults, the following example is included.

$$(datefile,daterequest) \rightarrow clientinfo$$
$$datefile \rightarrow dateinfo$$
$$(clientinfo,dateinfo) \rightarrow score$$
$$(dateinfo,score) \rightarrow bestmatch$$

FIGURE 6.14. Compressed data interfaces for *dater*.

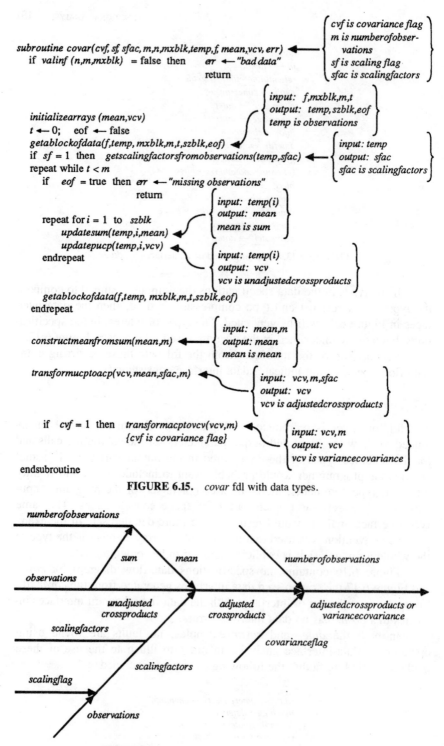

```
subroutine covar(cvf, sf, sfac, m,n,mxblk,temp,f, mean,vcv, err)  ◄── ⎧ cvf is covariance flag
    if valinf (n,m,mxblk) = false then      err ◄── "bad data"        ⎪ m is numberofobser-
                            return                                     ⎨     vations
                                                                       ⎪ sf is scaling flag
                                                                       ⎩ sfac is scalingfactors


    initializearrays (mean,vcv)                  ⎧ input: f,mxblk,m,t
    t ◄── 0;   eof ◄── false                     ⎨ output: temp,szblk,eof
    getablockofdata(f,temp, mxblk,m,t,szblk,eof) ◄── ⎩ temp is observations
    if sf = 1 then  getscalingfactorsfromobservations(temp,sfac) ◄── ⎧ input: temp
    repeat while t < m                                               ⎨ output: sfac
        if   eof = true then  err ◄── "missing observations"         ⎩ sfac is scalingfactors
                        return
                                                          ⎧ input: temp(i)
        repeat for i = 1 to  szblk                        ⎨ output: mean
            updatesum(temp,i,mean) ◄──                    ⎩ mean is sum
            updatepucp(temp,i,vcv) ◄──       ⎧ input: temp(i)
        endrepeat                            ⎨ output: vcv
                                             ⎩ vcv is unadjustedcrossproducts

        getablockofdata(f,temp, mxblk,m,t,szblk,eof)
    endrepeat
                                             ⎧ input: mean,m
    constructmeanfromsum(mean,m)  ◄──        ⎨ output: mean
                                             ⎩ mean is mean

    transformmucptoacp(vcv,mean,sfac,m)  ◄── ⎧ input: vcv,m,sfac
                                             ⎨ output: vcv
                                             ⎩ vcv is adjustedcrossproducts

    if  cvf = 1 then   transformacptovcv(vcv,m)  ◄── ⎧ input: vcv,m
                       {cvf is covariance flag}     ⎨ output: vcv
                                                     ⎩ vcv is variancecovariance
endsubroutine
```

FIGURE 6.15. *covar* fdl with data types.

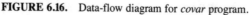

FIGURE 6.16. Data-flow diagram for *covar* program.

$(observations, scalingflag) \rightarrow scalingfactors$
$observations \rightarrow sum$
$observations \rightarrow unadjustedcrossproducts$
$(sum, numberofobservations) \rightarrow mean$
$(unadjustedcrossproducts, mean, scalingfactors) \rightarrow adjustedcrossproducts$
$(adjustedcrossproducts, covarianceflag, numberofobservations) \rightarrow variancecovariance$

FIGURE 6.17.   Type interfaces for *covar*.

6.7.3 Telegram Example

Figure 6.18 contains the fdl for a telegram counter program which has the following specification.

"The program is to read a sequence of words using the *getnextword* operator. The words belong to a sequence of telegrams. Each telegram is a sequence of words that ends with the special word "ZZZZ." The sequence of telegrams ends with the empty telegram. That is, the telegram contains only the word "ZZZZ." Some words are oversized and this is checked using the *oversize* function. The program is supposed to count the number of words in each telegram and to print this out along with a flag which specifies whether or not the telegram has an oversized word."

The data-flow specification for *telegramcounter* is contained in Figure 6.19 and the compressed data interfaces for the fdl are in Figure 6.20. Comparison of the two quickly reveals an inconsistency. The type *word* interfaces with the type *notspecialword* in the fdl, but in the data-flow diagram it interfaces with *notoversizeword*, which then interfaces with *notspecialword*. This interface failure is caused by a conditional statement subordination fault. The fdl if statement which checks to see if a word is special is not subordinated to the if statement which checks to see if it is oversize. The problem shows up in other ways as well. The fdl, for example, contains no mention of the types *specialword* and *notoversizeword*. The omission of *specialword*, on examination of the fdl, is seen not to matter, since this type does not lead anywhere. The omission of *notoversizeword* is associated with the condi-

```
function telegramcounter
     oversizewordflag ← false
     repeat until telegramwordcount = 0
     telegramwordcount ← 0
        repeat until word = "ZZZZ"
           word ← getnextword {getnextword uses telegramfile}
           if oversize(word) = true then {word is oversizeword}
                                          oversizewordflag ← true
           if special(word) = false
              then {word is notspecialword}
                       telegramwordcount ← telegramwordcount + 1
        endrepeat
        return(oversizewordflag, telegramwordcount)
     endrepeat
endfunction
```

FIGURE 6.18.   Fdl for *telegramcounter* with error.

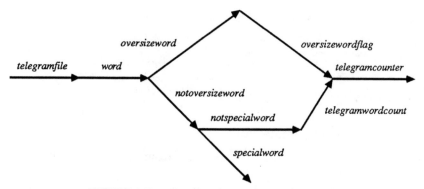

FIGURE 6.19.   Data-flow diagram for *telegramcounter*.

tional statement subordination problem in the same way as is the illegal interface.

There are several interfaces in the specifications diagram which are not in the set of data interfaces generated from the program. This is not due to faults, but occurs due to the way interfaces are generated. The interface

$$word \rightarrow notoversizeword$$

is implicitly present. To make it explicit the user would have to put an *else* branch for the conditional statement

$$if\ oversize(word) = true\ then\ldots$$

in order to insert a type comment in the appropriate place. An alternative is automatic type redefinition for conditionals in which the new types are generated from the function name used to test for the condition. This is equivalent to automatic generation of type comments for conditional statement classification. Thus, in this example, the condition function *oversize* could be used to automatically construct the two type redefinition comments

{*word is oversizeword*}   and   {*word is notoversizeword*}.

Although this idea will work for fdl's, it may not work for programs in general.

The exercise at the end of the chapter contains an example of an fdl containing a fault which can be found using operator-sequence analysis.

telegramfile → *word*
word → *oversizeword*
oversizeword → *oversizewordflag*
word → *notspecialword*
notspecialword → *telegramwordcount*
(*oversizewordflag,telegramwordcount*) → *telegramcounter*

FIGURE 6.20   Data interfaces for *telegramcounter*.

6.8 PROGRAM COMMENTS

Comments in programs are considered to be a necessary part of a program's documentation, and programmers are entreated to include them, but there has been little in the way of systematic guidelines describing what should be included. One of the advantages of operator-interface and data-interface analysis is that they specify what kinds of comments should be included in a program or fdl, and what kinds of analysis they can be used for. The comments required for operator and sequence analysis form the basis of good program documentation and should not be considered an added burden to the programmer. The two basic kinds of documentation comments are

{*operatorname*}   and   {*varname is typename*}.

In addition to these, there are the less general kinds, such as the input-output specifications for subroutines and the *uses* comment for identifying input data sources.

6.9 SUMMARY

Structural analysis looks for faults in which functions are joined together into incorrect structures. It is possible, in the manner of functional testing, to characterize classes of faults, and to define structural analysis methods which can be used to find those faults. A method which depends on the availability of a trace oracle was described which can be used to find missing statement faults.

Most structural analysis techniques are failure-analysis rather than fault-analysis methods. They look for failures in the interfaces between objects which occur along the paths that are traversed when a structure is executed. Three kinds of interface analysis were described.

The highest level of interface analysis, involving the interfaces between large system objects, is module-interface analysis. This includes examining the parameter lists of interacting functions for consistency. It also ensures that all called functions are actually defined.

At a lower level, data-interface analysis looks at transformations of one type of data into another inside a function or module. This kind of analysis depends on an external description of the correct or expected data transformations, which can be given in the form of a data-flow diagram. A data interface in a program occurs when one or more data types is used to generate data of another type. Data-interface analysis examines the data interfaces which occur in a program or fdl and compares them for consistency with the data interfaces in a specifications data-flow diagram. The types of data occurring in a program are recognized by the names of the variables in which they are stored or from comments which explicitly name the types of data stored in particular variables at selected places in a program.

Data-flow diagrams can be assumed to have a special property called "completely duplicated labels," which makes it possible to conclude that if all the interfaces in a program are contained in a specifications data-flow diagram, then the implicit data-flow graph in the program is a subgraph of the specifications diagram. This means if there are no interface failures, there are no data-flow sequence failures.

At the lowest level, operator-interface analysis examines data structure operators. There are two aspects to this. The first is to see that the data structure operators are applied to objects of the appropriate type. The second concerns legal sequences of operators. Data structure operators can usually occur only in restricted kinds of sequences. These can be specified in a legal sequences graph in which the nodes are operators. Operator-interface analysis identifies all pairs of operators (f,g) in the program where operator f is followed by operator g without any intervening operator, and examines the legal sequences diagram to confirm that this operator interface is legal, or that operator f can be followed by operator g. Operator-interface analysis can also be done for determining the legality of larger program operator sequences than pairs but, because of the Markov property of legal sequences graphs, interface analysis can be proved to be sufficient. The method may, like data-interface analysis, require embedded program comments. In this case they are needed to identify operators for which there are no explicit programming language constructs or defined functions. Operator-interface analysis must be carried out separately for each data structure and its operations, but the analyses can be done in parallel.

The comments required in operator and interface analysis can be used as the basis for a systematic approach to program documentation.

EXERCISES

6.1. Construct a legal sequences diagram for the *push* and *pop* operators for a stack which indicates that all operator sequences must begin with one or more *push* operators.

6.2. Review the ways in which type transformations can occur in a program or fdl and list each of these.

6.3. Expand the data-flow specification in Figure 6.12 for the dating function to include the additional data type *bdate* from the *dater* fdl in Figure 6.10.

6.4. For the *covar* fdl in Figure 6.15, construct a complete list of type comments for its parameters. From this generate a data interfaces description for the subroutine taken as a whole, showing which kinds of input data are transformed into which kinds of output data.

6.5. Figure 6.21 contains the fdl for a program which has the following specification.

"The program is to read the complete sequence of records from the file *accntfile*. The file is sorted by account number and contains two kinds of rec-

```
function accountupdate
    initializeaccntfile
    if endaccntfile = true then return("error: empty file")
    accntrecord ← getnextaccntrecord {getnextaccnt uses accntfile}
    if nonfinancial(accntrecord) = true then output(accntinfo(accntrecord))
                                        else subtotal ← debit(accntrecord)
    lastaccnt ← accntnum(accntrecord) {initializebreakdata}
    repeat while endaccntfile = true
        accntrecord ← getnextaccntrecord
        if nonfinancial(accnt) = true
            then output(accntinfo(accntrecord))
            else if lastaccnt ≠ accntnumber(accntrecord) {checkbreak-
data}
                then output(lastaccnt,subtotal)
                    subtotal ← 0
                else subtotal ← subtotal + debit(accntrecord)
        lastaccnt ← accntnum(accntrecord) {updatebreakdata}
    endrepeat
    output(lastaccnt,subtotal)
endfunction
```

FIGURE 6.21. Fdl for *accountupdate* program.

ords: *financial* and *nonfinancial*. There may be several records of both types for each account. Certain kinds of information in each nonfinancial record are printed out without further analysis. For each account's financial records, the debit amounts in the records are totaled and then printed out."

The fdl contains a number of data structures and associated operators which are listed below. Note that comments have been included in the program to identify the application of the break-data data structure operators since these are not explicit program functions.

(1) data structure: *accntfile*
    operators: *initializeaccntfile, endacctfile, getnextaccntrecord*
(2) data structure: *breakdata*
    operators: *checkbreakdata, updatebreakdata*
(3) data structure: *subtotal*
    operators: *initializesubtotal, updatesubtotal*

Figure 6.22 contains the legal sequences diagram for *breakdata*. Construct legal sequences diagrams for the other data structures and carry out an operator sequences analysis of the design to determine the presence of any operator interface failures.

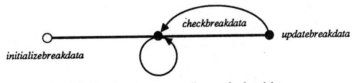

checkbreakdata

updatebreakdata

initializebreakdata

FIGURE 6.22. Legal sequences diagram for *breakdata*.

6.6. Construct a data-flow diagram which describes the principal data transformations which are carried out in the *accountupdate* fdl in Exercise 6.5.

REFERENCES

1. B. W. Boehm, R. K. McClean, and D. B. Urfig, Some experience with aids to the design of large-scale software, *IEEE Transactions on Software Engineering*, vol. SE-1, 1, 1975.
2. W. E. Howden, Applicability of software validation techniques to scientific programs, *ACM Transactions on Programming Languages and Systems*, vol. 2, 3, 1980.
3. L. Werner (private communication), 1986.

CHAPTER
7

MANAGEMENT
AND
PLANNING

7.1 INTRODUCTION

The preceding chapters of the book have concentrated on the establishment
of a philosophy of program testing and on the methods needed to implement
it. The mathematical foundations and supporting tools for particular techniques have been described, but there has been no discussion of how to manage the testing and analysis activity. This chapter discusses management and
planning. It describes different ways to organize the testing effort, additional
testing terminology, and levels of testing. Three levels of testing and analysis are described, which include increasingly more complex techniques and
more extensive use of tools.

7.2 LIFE-CYCLE MANAGEMENT

One way of decomposing and organizing the testing effort is according to
the stages of the classical software life cycle.[1] This is a natural decomposition for the approach described in this book since it involves the different
products of the cycle. The validation activities that should take place in each
phase correspond to the documents used and produced by that phase.

159

Recall that the software life-cycle model is an idealized description of the relationship between different software development products. It is not being suggested that software development always proceeds from requirements, to design, to detailed design, to programming, or even that it contains all of these phases. It may not be possible to pin down requirements until after detailed design. There may be no need for requirements, or it may be possible to proceed directly from general design to coding. For very specialized applications, it may be possible to automatically generate code directly from formal requirements specifications. The life-cycle model is used for categorizing different kinds of software development products and general relationships between them. For this purpose it is a good model.

The testing and analysis activities associated with requirements include the identification of the basic functions and basic types of data in the requirements and their interrelationships. The relationships can be modeled using data-flow diagrams. Functional testing requires that the code implementing each of these functions be tested. Functional analysis can be used to confirm that data-type interfaces in detailed designs and code are consistent with the data and function relationships described in the data-flow diagrams.

Testing and analysis methods involving general design also depend on function and data identification. General design module-interface specifications can be compared for consistency amongst themselves and with more detailed module descriptions produced in later life-cycle phases. If data abstractions are used in this phase, operator-sequence diagrams should be produced which can be used to analyze fdl's and programs for legal sequences of operations. Structure diagrams produced at this stage can be compared for data-flow consistency with requirements data-flow diagrams.

Detailed design function and data definitions will also be used in testing and analysis. Like requirements and general design functions, detailed design function implementations will have to be tested. Module-interface analysis will have to be carried out for new modules introduced at this stage and also for modules previously defined for which more detailed descriptions have been given. Operator-sequence diagrams must be produced for all data structures introduced at this point to allow legal sequence analysis in both fdl algorithm descriptions and programs. Fdl designs may include comments if these are necessary to do operator-sequence analysis and data-interface analysis. The function and data descriptions produced at each life-cycle phase can be compared with those produced in other phases.

Once programming has been completed, a complete set of functional tests and analyses can be carried out. In order to do this it may be necessary to include extra code in the program in order to monitor intermediate-level functions that correspond to parts of programs. Operator-sequence analysis can be carried out for low-level problem-independent data structure operators such as assigning to and referencing a variable, and opening, accessing, and closing a file. Operator-sequence analysis can also be carried out for higher-level data structure operators whose legal sequence diagrams were produced during design. Data-interface analysis of the type that can be done for detailed designs can also be performed. This may require the insertion of type identification comments. Symbolic evaluation may be useful for testing code which implements functions whose specifications are functional formulae like those for the *covar* example.

Figure 7.1 gives an overall view of life-cycle testing and validation activities.

7.3 MODULE, INTEGRATION, AND ACCEPTANCE TESTING

Testing is often organized around the structure of a program or system rather than the development products of the life cycle. First individual modules or programs are tested during *unit testing*. This is followed by *integration testing*, in which interacting collections of modules are tested together. Finally, during *system* and *acceptance testing* the entire system is tested.

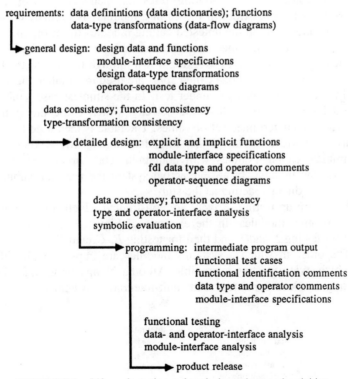

requirements: data definintions (data dictionaries); functions
data-type transformations (data-flow diagrams)

general design: design data and functions
module-interface specifications
design data-type transformations
operator-sequence diagrams

data consistency; function consistency
type-transformation consistency

detailed design: explicit and implicit functions
module-interface specifications
fdl data type and operator comments
operator-sequence diagrams

data consistency; function consistency
type and operator-interface analysis
symbolic evaluation

programming: intermediate program output
functional test cases
functional identification comments
data type and operator comments
module-interface specifications

functional testing
data- and operator-interface analysis
module-interface analysis

product release

FIGURE 7.1. Life-cycle testing and analysis products and activities.

The test and analysis materials that are prepared during the life cycle have different degrees of importance for the three kinds of testing. In system and acceptance testing and analysis, the details of module interaction and of individual pieces of code are ignored; it is primarily the system requirements that are used. In integration testing, module interaction is examined and there is a strong association with general design. Unit testing concentrates on individual pieces of code so that the detailed design and code are the most important. This relationship between life-cycle products and the organization of program testing and analysis is described in Figure 7.2.

7.4 BOTTOM-UP AND TOP-DOWN TESTING

Another topic often included in any discussion of testing and analysis is *bottom-up* versus *top-down* testing. Suppose that a tree is constructed that shows the call or usage relationships between modules, as in Figure 7.3. Module A at the top calls other modules but is not called by any other module. If it is tested first, as in top-down testing, then some way of isolating it from possible errors in the untested modules at lower levels must be used. Alternatively, module E calls no other modules but is called by other modules. If it is tested first, as in bottom-up testing, then some way of calling it which isolates it from errors in the calling modules is needed, in order to avoid mistaking errors in the untested calling modules for errors in E.

In top-down testing, modules are examined starting from the top of the call structure tree and then by working down through the tree to the bottom modules. Small pieces of code called *stubs* are used to simulate the modules called by the module currently under test. In the simplest case, stubs simulate modules using tables. Tests are selected which cause the stub to be called with a predetermined set of values. The table is then used by the stub to return the correct output for the simulated module. More complex stubs may simulate called modules with nontabular code or may even be prototypes for the module. In an interactive system the user can simulate the called module directly, acting as the stub.

In bottom-up testing, *drivers* are constructed which simulate modules which call other modules. In the example of Figure 7.3, a driver will be needed for testing E and F and then for testing B, C, and D.

The order in which a system's modules are implemented will determine which style of testing is possible. All other things being equal, bottom-up testing is more consistent with unit-integration-system testing. It also

	unit	integration	system
requirements	*	*	*
general design	*	*	
detailed design	*	*	
programming	*		

FIGURE 7.2. Life-cycle documents and program testing and analysis.

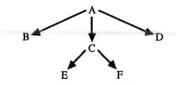

FIGURE 7.3. Module call graph.

does not require the development of stubs, which is in principle more difficult than constructing drivers. For this reason bottom-up testing is recommended. The exception to this is the use of top-down testing early in software development to test top-level modules such as, for example, user interfaces and process schedulers.

7.5 LEVELS OF TESTING AND ANALYSIS

Functional testing and analysis utilizes both human and machine resources, and it may be necessary to limit it to a subset of the methods described in the earlier chapters of the book. Three levels of testing ranging from the most basic to the most complex have been identified.

7.5.1 α-Testing and Analysis

The most basic level of testing and analysis involves both functional testing and analysis, but no automated tools are used. It is similar to the style of testing and analysis that has been practiced informally for many years. The difference is that a rationale is available to guide the activities.

In α-testing, the user identifies functions to be tested either from requirements, design and code documents, or from code documents alone. The necessary output statements are inserted into code to allow the observation of variable values that correspond to function input and output, and test data is selected based on informal rules such as "test all boundary values or extremal cases." The theoretical rationale for these rules is to indirectly cause the testing of Boolean conditions associated with conditional and iterative syntheses over the required fault-revealing data. No attempt is made to ensure that boundary input and output for functions really do correspond to the required values for the Booleans embedded in a function's code.

In α-analysis, the code and/or detailed design is manually read to check the flow of control and data. Data is examined to observe if it goes through the expected transformations. Checks are made to see that input-output devices and data structures are properly initialized and accessed, and closed if appropriate. The goal is to verify that no data-flow or operator-sequence failures can occur. Structured walk-through[2] may be used to organize the analysis activities.

7.5.2   β-Testing and Analysis

This middle level of testing requires more of the analyst and depends on the use of several tools. It is easily achievable using current technology and does not depend on any ideas for which there is no substantial body of experience.

The goal in β-testing is to carry out the same kind of functional testing as in α-testing, but to use a tool to check to see if all functions have been tested and none forgotten. This is not completely achievable but some measure of confidence can be had with a simple check such as branch or LCJS[3] testing. A tool is used to allow the programmer to confirm that all branches, or similar elementary program constructs, have been executed on at least one test.

In β-analysis, simple automated tools are used to assist with structural-analysis methods that are easy to automate but difficult to do manually. The simplest is the use of a tool which checks for references to undefined variables. A tool could also be used for other simple operator sequences, such as the open-read-write-close sequences for files. β-analysis also requires that the user insert comments to denote data types and flavors in order to assist manual data-flow analysis.

7.5.3   γ-Testing and Analysis

This is the highest level of functional testing and analysis, and contains most of the methods described in the book. Some of the methods have not been extensively used, and significant effort may be required to implement them.

The goal in γ-testing is to use tools to force the testing of all functions over all common fault-revealing test data. This requires the use of two kinds of tools. The first tool is used to determine if all functions have been tested. Either dr-chains or data-context data-flow analysis can be used. The assumption is that functions correspond to data-flow patterns. This goal can only be approximated and only 1dr- (data reference) or 1dc- (data context) testing is suggested.

The second tool required in γ-level functional testing is a coverage tool to determine if functions have been tested over appropriate fault-revealing data. This is approximated using a testing tool that monitors the kinds of data over which individual statements and branches are executed. The tool will ensure that all Boolean branching statements are executed over the types of tests needed to reveal simple conditional and iterative synthesis faults. It can also be used to ensure that expressions are tested over expression fault-revealing tests. The required kinds of tests are discussed in Chapter 5.

In addition, γ-testing may also incorporate a symbolic evaluator to be used for expression-synthesis analysis and infeasible path detection. The infeasible path capabilities can be used to filter out infeasible dr- and dc-chains in a program.

Both α- and β-testing concentrate on code testing. In γ-level functional testing it is expected that functional fdl's will be used in detailed design and will also be tested using an fdl symbolic evaluator.

The tools required for γ-analysis include an automated operator-sequence analyzer like that described for β-analysis. The difference is that it will be capable of doing operator-sequence analysis for operators not implemented directly by explicit programming language operations. This will require that the user put comments in his program that identify implicit operators, and which can be automatically recognized by the operator-sequence analysis tool.

γ-analysis requires a data-flow analysis tool for comparing data-flow specifications with code. The code will have to be documented with comments such as those described in Chapter 6 in order to allow recognition of implicit data types and flavors. In addition, a data-flow analysis tool should be available for verification of data flow in detailed design fdl's.

The three levels of testing, and the methods and tools they involve, are summarized in Figure 7.4.

7.6 SOFTWARE ENGINEERING DATABASES

The management of a software development project involves keeping track of software development products and their interdependencies. This includes requirements, design, and code documents. Testing and analysis objects include test cases, test output, coverage results and summaries, dynamic assertion violations, data type analysis results, and operator sequence analysis results. A software engineering database would be useful both for software

α-*testing*
- input/output extremal values for functional testing
- random nonextremal tests

α-*analysis*
- code reading for data transformations and operator sequences

β-*testing*
- input/output extremal values for functional testing
- branch coverage tool

β-*analysis*
- code reading for data transformations
- use of flavor comments
- operator-sequence analysis tool for undefined variables, device, and file operations

γ-*testing*
- expression, conditional, and iterative synthesis fault-revealing test data coverage tool
- data-flow analysis tool for function detection
- symbolic evaluation for testing and infeasibility analysis
- symbolic evaluation tool for fdl's

γ-*analysis*
- automated data-transform analysis tool which uses type comments and data-flow specifications
- operator-sequence analysis tool for explicit and implicit operators
- automated data-transformation analysis tool for machine readable fdl's

FIGURE 7.4. Levels of functional testing and analysis.

development and testing and analysis, as well as maintenance, and version management and control. Software engineering databases is still a research area, but the basic features of a system that would be useful for functional testing and analysis can be easily identified.

The relational data model could be used to design the internal structure of a software development database. Recall that in the relational model, the database consists of a set of relational tables resembling indexed files. Each entry or row in the table contains a set of objects which have the relationship associated with the table. The entries, or rows of the table, can be accessed according to the contents of specified row positions. The database contains facilities for manipulating tables for the storage and retrieval of information.

Figure 7.5 contains examples of the types of relational tables that might occur in a functional test and analysis data base. The first table, or relation, relates test output results with test cases and program modules. The second relates the branch coverage statistics of individual tests to tested modules. The third relates fdl detailed designs and data-flow diagrams to data-type transformation analyses in which the diagram is used to analyze the associated fdl. The fourth table gives the branch coverage summaries for each program module. It is derived by combining all of the branch coverage information for a module from the rows of a table like that in part (b) of the figure.

A software engineering database will have to interface both directly with the user and with other software development tools. The user interface will allow the user to enter, edit, and delete objects and relationships. A user-oriented system can be constructed which knows about all the different kinds of possible objects and relationships. A menu-driven interface, or an interface which automatically checks the syntax and form of entered information, could be used. The user interface may contain a number of data entry tools, including graphics facilities.

Testing and analysis tools which use objects in the database to produce other objects are called *data generation* tools. A functional testing tool, for example, will use program and test case objects to produce test result objects. In general, each testing or analysis data generation tool will be associated with a relational database relation which records the results of its application. *Data summary* tools present stored information to users in a readable format.

The use of a software engineering database makes many software development tasks easier and eliminates the need for a variety of special purpose software tools. Regression testing, for example, becomes much easier. A regression tool can easily be built which accesses the previously run test cases for a program, retests the program against them, and generates new test result relations. A test results operator can be used to compare the test results for different versions of a program, and a data summary tool to generate regression testing reports for the user.

program module	testcase	test output
. . .	. . .	. . .

(*a*)

program module	testcase	branch coverage
. . .	. . .	. . .

(*b*)

fdl description	data-flow diagram	data-type analysis results
. . .	. . .	. . .

(*c*)

program module	branch coverage summary
. . .	. . .

(*d*)

FIGURE 7.5.   Examples of software engineering database relations. (*a*) Test output results. (*b*) Test coverage results. (*c*) Data-flow analysis results. (*d*) Branch coverage summaries.

7.7 SUMMARY

Software testing and analysis activities can be classified using the software life cycle. Different activities are associated with different life-cycle documents (e.g., requirements data-flow diagrams, code, structure diagrams, etc.). Testing and analysis can also be broken down into unit, integration, and system validation. This can be used to organize validation during the final testing and analysis stages. The life-cycle decomposition is a breakdown of earlier activities in preparation for validation. Note that this is an idealized decomposition since software construction is rarely a straightforward process. Some code may be finished before other code has been designed. Requirements may be found during detailed design to be inadequate, and then rewritten.

Top-down testing and analysis is appropriate in the earlier stages of development, in which top-level driver modules, or user interfaces, may be developed first. Bottom-up testing is appropriate during the later stages when all modules are available.

Three levels of testing, α-, β-, and γ-functional testing and analysis, were identified. In α-testing, manual techniques are used to test program functions over good functional test data and to analyze programs for data-type and operator-sequencing failures. No tools are used except for a database for storing and retrieving programs and test cases. In β-testing, tools are introduced to help automate functional testing and analysis. A minimal set of tools includes a coverage analyzer to ensure that all functional components have been tested, and elementary tools for operator- and data-type-sequence analysis. The minimal operator-sequence analysis tool is one which can be used to analyze a program for correct sequences of assignments and references (a variable must be assigned a value before it can be referenced). Other generic kinds of operations might also be analyzed, such as file operations (e.g., a file must be opened before it can be read). β-testing may also include the use of a test harness or dynamic assertions for automatically checking the output from a set of functional tests.

The goal in γ-testing is to automate functional testing and analysis as completely as possible. Data-flow analysis tools using data-reference chains or data contexts are used to identify functions in order to ensure that all functions are tested. Test coverage tools keep track of the types of data over which program statements (i.e., function synthesizers) have been executed in order to see if functions have been tested over fault-revealing test data. Automated tools for structural analysis are included which can compare data-flow specifications with fdl detailed designs and program code to determine correctness of data-type transformations. Operator-sequence analysis tools are also included.

A software engineering database can be used to manage software development products, such as tests, programs, and design specifications, and their interdependencies. Software tools can be built to operate on and produce new objects in the database. A relational database with suitable tool and user interfaces would be sufficient.

EXERCISES

7.1. Simulate α, β, and γ levels of functional testing and analysis for the *dater* fdl in Figure 6.10.

7.2. Simulate α, β, and γ levels of functional testing and analysis for the *covar* fdl in Figure 6.15.

7.3. Construct examples of possible errors in the *dater* function whose fdl appears in Figure 6.10 which:

   (a) would be found by γ-testing and analysis but not α- or β-testing and analysis,

(b) would be found by β-testing and analysis but not α-testing and analysis,

(c) would be found by α-testing and analysis.

7.4. Repeat Exercise 7.3 for the *covar* function whose fdl appears in Figure 6.15.

7.5. Construct an example of a simple inventory control system. Construct a complete set of data-flow requirements and a structured design. Provide fdl detailed design descriptions for the algorithms. Make a list of all functions embedded in the system and all data types and data transformations. Verify the fdl against the data transformation descriptions and construct functional fdl test data using the techniques for functional testing described in Chapter 5.

REFERENCES

1. W. E. Howden, Life cycle software validation, *Computer*, vol. 15, 2, 1982.
2. E. Yourdon, *Structured Walkthroughs*, Yourdon Press, New York, 1978.
3. M. R. Woodward, D. Hedley, and M. A. Hennell, Experience with path analysis and testing of programs, *IEEE Transactions on Software Engineering*, vol. 6, 13, 1980.

INDEX